ORIGAMI
SCULPTURES

Second Edition

Other books by John Montroll:

Origami Sea Life by John Montroll and Robert Lang

Prehistoric Origami *Dinosaurs and Other Creatures*

African Animals in Origami

Animal Origami for the Enthusiast

Origami for the Enthusiast

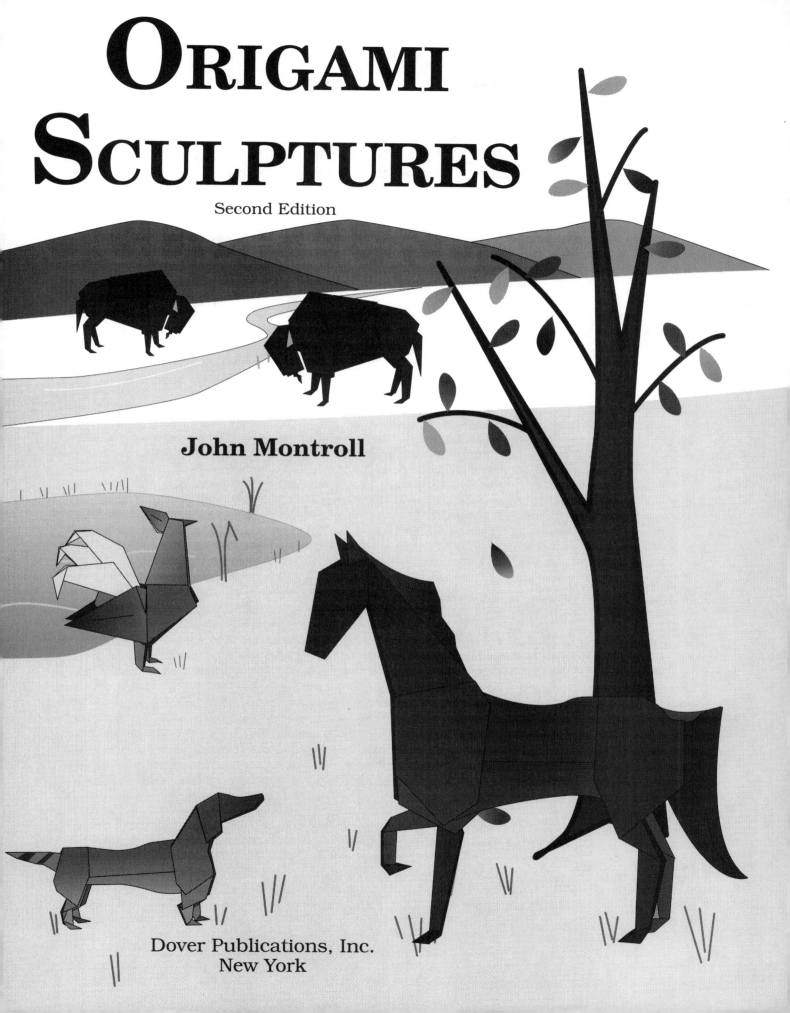

ORIGAMI SCULPTURES

Second Edition

John Montroll

Dover Publications, Inc.
New York

To Jeremy, Rachel, and Josh

Copyright © 1990 by John Montroll.
All rights reserved under Pan American and International Copyright Conventions.

Published in Canada by General Publishing Company, Ltd., 30 Lesmill Road, Don Mills, Toronto, Ontario.
Published in the United Kingdom by Constable and Company, Ltd., 3 The Lanchesters, 162–164 Fulham Palace Road, London W6 9ER.

This Dover edition, first published in 1990, is an unabridged and unaltered republication of the second edition of the work originally published in 1990 by Antroll Publishing Company, Vermont.

Manufactured in the United States of America
Dover Publications, Inc., 31 East 2nd Street, Mineola, N.Y. 11501

Library of Congress Cataloging-in-Publication Data

Montroll, John.
    Origami sculptures / John Montroll.
      p.   cm.
    Reprint. Originally published: 2nd ed. Vermont: Antroll Pub. Co., c1990.
    ISBN 0-486-26587-0 (pbk.)
    1. Origami.   I. Title.
TT870.M57   1990b
736'.982—dc20
                                 90-13972
                                     CIP

Introduction

This book represents a new direction in origami for me. First, I have made liberal use of new bases that I have recently created, including Montroll's base and the insect base, which allow me to fold models that are very similar to their real life counterparts. Also, several of the models in this book are folded in such a way as to bring out their three dimensional characteristics. And finally, in preparing this book on origami I have made use of the latest in computer technology, thus blending an art of the past with the scientific horizon of the future. This entire manuscript was generated on a graphics computer, and each page was printed on a state of the art laser printer.

The style of origami presented in this book is the square-sheet, no-cutting method, with the exception of the Walrus, which is to be folded from a dollar bill. The directions for folding the models follow the Randlett-Yoshizawa method of instruction, with some of my own modifications.

For those new to origami, I have included a section that teaches the basic folds that will be utilized in my models. The first four models are designed to introduce the beginner to origami. In addition, each model is accompanied with notes.

Since most origami paper is colored on one side and white on the other, proper shading for each model is indicated by actual shading in the directions. The shading represents the colored side of the paper. This will be important in such models as the Panda and Penguin where the shading becomes an integral part of the model's design.

Although any square sheet of paper can be used in folding these models, the best results come from using standard origami paper. Origami paper can be found at many hobby shops, or purchased from the Friends of The Origami Center of America. The Friends is a tax exempt national organization committed to the sharing of paper folding. For more information about the Friends (books and supplies), send a self-addressed business size envelope with two first class stamps to:

The Friends of The Origami Center of America
15 West, 77th Street
New York, NY 10024

Origami paper, and a catalog of other available craft books, can also be ordered from Dover Publications, Inc., at:

Dover Publications, Inc.
31 East 2nd St.
Mineola, NY 11501

I wish to thank the following people for their valuble contribution. Robert Lang helped in several ways. As this entire manuscript was generated by a graphics computer, Robert Lang wrote computer programs which enabled me to draw very clear and aesthetically pleasing styles of lines. He also wrote the article on the history of origami. I thank him for his fine work. Also, I thank my brother Andy for his continued help in the design of this book.

John Montroll

Contents

Husky
***
Page 57

Penguin
***
Page 61

Peacock
***
Page 65

Horse
***
Page 71

Bison
***
Page 73

Camel
***
Page 76

Dromedary
***
Page 80

Rhinoceros
***
Page 84

Weevil
****
Page 96

Asparagus Beetle
****
Page 100

Panda
***
Page 103

Elephant
***
Page 110

Contents 7

A Brief History of Origami

Origami, a Japanese word meaning "folded paper," is an art closely associated with Japanese culture. It actually originated in China, however, as did the manufacture of paper. Buddhist monks brought the art of paper-making to Japan in the sixth century, and, it is thought, brought the simplest origami designs as well. Over the next few centuries, while paperfolding languished in China, it flourished in Japan.

Paper was initially a precious commodity, affordable only by the nobility, and was therefore used only for ceremonial purposes. Among the nobility, gifts would be decorated with *noshi*, pleated squares of paper filled with strips of dried abalone; at weddings, the bride and groom's cups of *sake* would be decorated with male and female paper butterflies. Because of its rarity, all paper was held as something sacred; this reverence continues even to this day. The Japanese words for "paper" and "God," though written with different symbols, are pronounced the same, *kami*.

Paper was incorporated into the national religion, Shinto, and paper objects became a part of its ceremonies. Inside Shinto shrines are paper streamers called *go-hei*, which indicate the presence of the deity; folded human figures, called *katashiro* are placed in shrines to receive the deity. The sacred designs tend to be highly stylized, and their folding sequences are rigidly defined.

In addition to the ceremonial designs, many recreational paper folds were also developed. These were passed down through the generations, primarily from mother to daughter. Because they were passed down by demonstration, only the simplest designs persisted for more than a generation or two. Written instructions exist only as far back as 1797, when two works, *Orikata Tehon Chishingura* and *Sembazuru Orikata* were published in the same year.

The term "origami" was introduced in the 1880s. It is composed from the Japanese word "*oru*," meaning "to fold," and "*kami*," paper. Prior to this time, the art had been called "*orisue*" or "*orikata.*"

While its ceremonial function was well established, the adoption of origami as a widespread recreation by the Japanese arose from their embrace of a Western cultural phenomenon. In the 1890s, the Japanese government established a Western-style system of primary education throughout the country, including kindergartens modeled on those of the German educator, Freidrich Fröbel. Fröbel was a strong proponent of paperfolding as a means of building hand-eye coordination, and his ideas met with a wide acceptance in Japan that continues today (one of the larger publishers of children's books is called *Froebel-kan*). Origami is taught throughout the primary schools of Japan and is a widely popular folk art, supported by both government and industry.

Origami spread beyond Japan, over a millenium ago. The Arabs brought the art of paper making to North Africa, and Muslim Moors brought it and paperfolding to Spain when they invaded in the eighth century A.D. They were expelled in the Spanish Inquisition of the Middle Ages, but they left behind their own tradition of geometric paper folds. This became the basis for a Spanish style of folding, or *papiroflexia*. The figures were originally geometric—for Islam forbade the making of images—but after the Moors were driven out, the tradition branched out into representational designs, and a strong school of folding exists today in Spain and Argentina.Very likely, wherever there has been paper, there has been paperfolding, for in nearly every culture that uses paper, there is some paperfolding tradition. American schoolchildren fold a toy they call a cootie-catcher; their British counterparts make the same shape and call it a fortune-teller or a salt cellar. Even the paper airplane has an illustrious history and can be found in the pages of Leonardo da Vinci's *Codex Atlanticus*. Simple paper toys are to be found in the East and West, but the evolution of origami into something beyond simple toys and stylized designs began in Japan only in the last century.

In the 1930s and 40s, a Japanese metalworker named Akira Yoshizawa began to create his own origami designs. Over the next 50 years, he folded tens of thousands of models and created hundreds of new designs. Equally important, he developed a code of lines and arrows to record the folding sequence for his designs and published several books, which served to standardize his notation over several other competing codes. In the 1950s and 1960s, his work caught on in the West and served as the inspiration for a new generation of folders. In America and Europe, new organizations grew up devoted to origami, and folders on both continents began to invent their own designs and in doing so, took the art in entirely new directions.

In fact, by the mid-1960s, the art was developing as fast in the West as it was in Japan. One of the modern developments was the restriction of the art; contrary to widespread belief, the traditional Japanese designs often used cuts, non-square or multiple sheets of paper. But, as origami designers' abilities improved, there arose an unofficial set of rules governing what was allowed and what wasn't, particularly in the West. In general, an origami figure from an uncut sheet was better than one from a cut sheet; a single sheet was more desirable than two; and a fold from a square was preferred over any other starting shape. This hierarchy was not so firmly established in Japan, where the use of multiple pieces is common and, for example, one master insists that the best starting shape is a $1:\sqrt{2}$ rectangle—but there is widespread consensus in the West that there is a purest form of origami, and this can be summed up as: one square, no cuts.

Within these rigid limitations, the art has grown to previously undreamed-of levels of sophistication. Today, there are origami masters around the world, and the designs they develop are continually expanding the boundaries of the art. There was a time when an origami designer might claim a particular subject impossible. Far too many "impossible" subjects have been folded for anyone to say that today. Birds, flowers, mammals, fish, crustacea, insects, people, machines, and abstract shapes, all flow from that simplest, most regular of shapes: the square.

Robert Lang

Symbols

Lines

– – – – – – – – – – Valley fold, fold in front.

– · – · – · – · – · – Mountain fold, fold behind.

———————— Crease line.

······················ X-ray or guide line.

Arrows

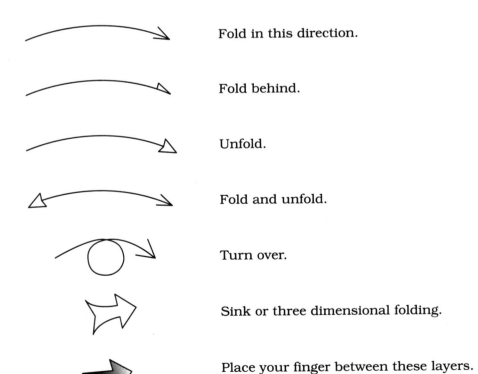

Fold in this direction.

Fold behind.

Unfold.

Fold and unfold.

Turn over.

Sink or three dimensional folding.

Place your finger between these layers.

Swan

The swan is the most graceful of birds. It is four to six feet long and feeds on aquatic vegetation in shallow water. On the water swans are quiet, but in flight they honk.

Two descriptions of the method for folding the swan are presented here. The first description presents every step in detail, the second presents the standard method of instructions, with details left to the experienced folder. In addition, the rabbit ear and outside reverse folds are introduced.

Method 1
The detailed way

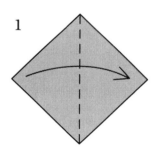

1

Begin with the colored side face up. Fold in half.

2

Unfold.

3

Turn over.

4

Kite-fold.

5

Fold up.

6

7

Unfold.

8

Fold up in the other direction.

9

Unfold.

10

Fold both sides to the center.

11

Unfold.

12

Fold both sides to the center.

13

Unfold.

17

Repeat steps 14–16 on the right.

16

This is another intermediate step. The rabbit ear is almost finished.

15

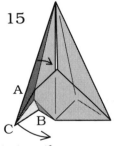

This is a three-dimensional intermediate step. Continue by folding C down.

14

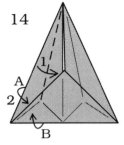

A rabbit ear fold will now be formed. Using the existing creases, fold the long part in half (arrow 1) while placing A and B together (arrow 2).

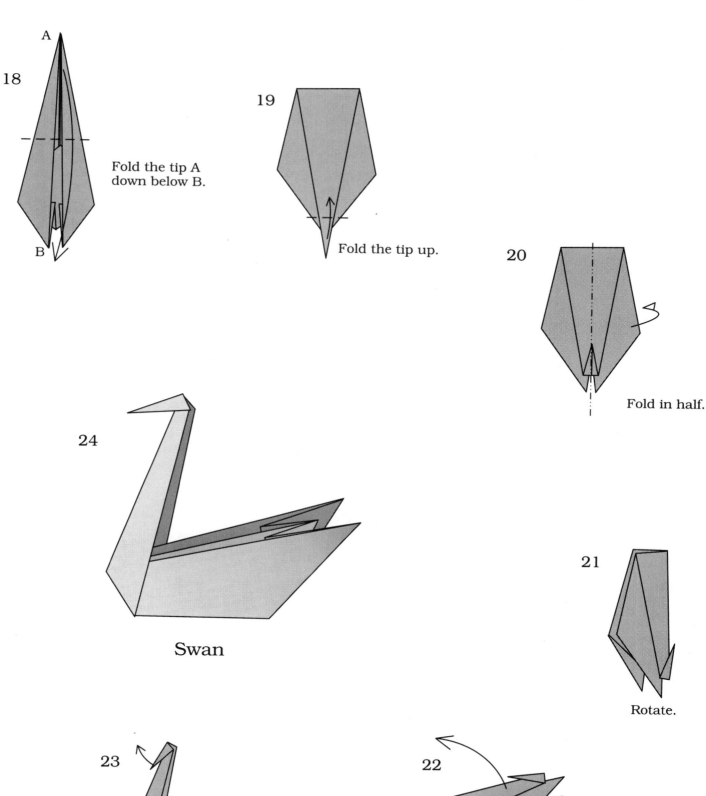

18

A

Fold the tip A
down below B.

B

19

Fold the tip up.

20

Fold in half.

24

Swan

21

Rotate.

23

Slide the head up.

22

Slide the neck up.

Method 2
The standard way

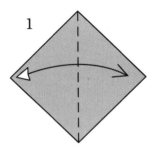

1

Fold, unfold
and turn over.

2

Kite-fold.

3

4

Rabbit-ear.

9

Swan

5

Rabbit-ear again.

8

Outside-reverse-fold
to form the head.

7

Outside-reverse-fold
to form the neck.

6

Fold in half
and rotate.

Diamond

This three-dimensional geometric shape makes an elegant ornament. It is formed from the Preliminary Fold, which is a common starting shape for many origami designs. A detailed method for making the Preliminary Fold is shown.

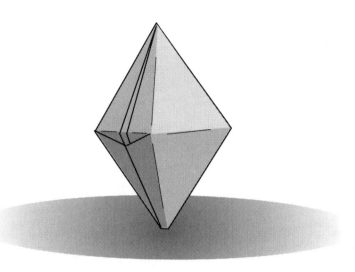

Steps 1 to 12 introduce the Preliminary Fold.

1

2

Unfold.

3

4

Unfold.

5

Turn over.

6

7

Unfold.

8

9

Unfold.

10

Collapse the model using the creases. Bring A, B, and C to D.

11

This is a three-dimensional intermediate step.

12

This is the Preliminary fold.

13

14

15

16

17

Unfold.

18

Unfold.

19

Fold A to B.

20

Unfold.

21

22

Repeat steps 13 to 18.

23

Fold A to the right and B behind to the left.

24

Repeat steps 14 to 18 on the front and back.

25

26

Repeat behind.

27

Use A as a guide.

28

Unfold.

29

30

Unfold.

31

32

Tuck inside.

33

Repeat steps 27 to 32 on the right and back.

34

Blow into the bottom to inflate the diamond.

35

Diamond

Tetrahedron

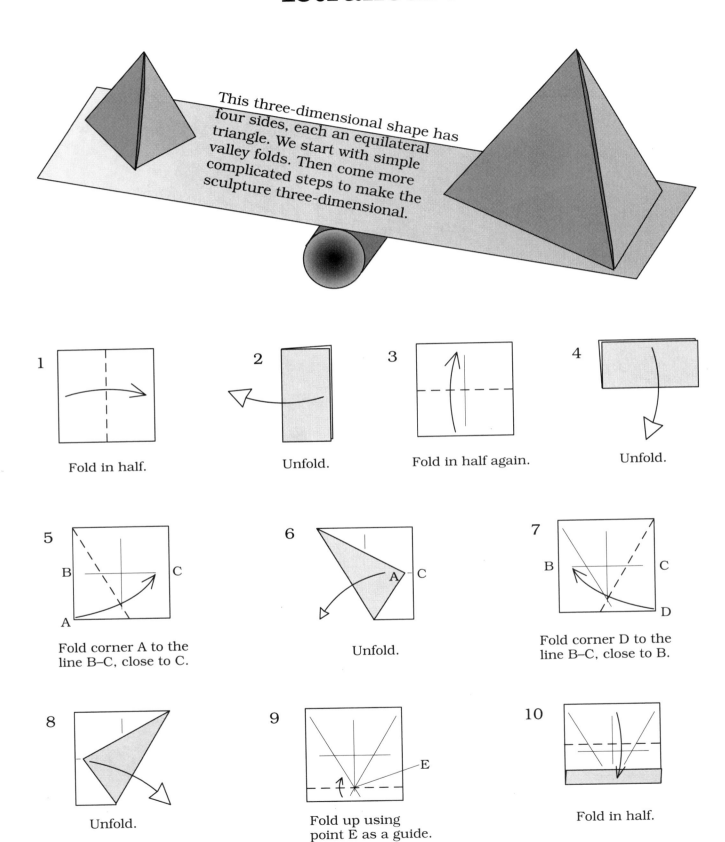

This three-dimensional shape has four sides, each an equilateral triangle. We start with simple valley folds. Then come more complicated steps to make the sculpture three-dimensional.

1 Fold in half.

2 Unfold.

3 Fold in half again.

4 Unfold.

5 Fold corner A to the line B–C, close to C.

6 Unfold.

7 Fold corner D to the line B–C, close to B.

8 Unfold.

9 Fold up using point E as a guide.

10 Fold in half.

11

Unfold.

12

Fold corner A to the line B–C, close to C.

13

14

Unfold.

15

Unfold.

16

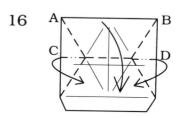

While folding the line A–B down, fold the edges C and D inside. Fold on the existing creases.

17

This is a three-dimensional intermediate step.

18

Lift C up. Bring A and B together.

19

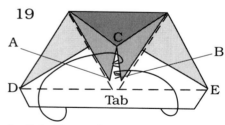

In this three-dimensional drawing, corner C is coming out of the page. Fold D and E up to C and tuck the long tab inside.

20

Tetrahedron

Octahedron

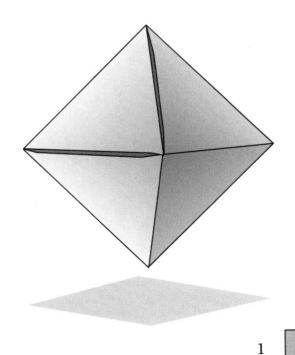

This three-dimensional shape has eight sides, each an equilateral triangle. The folding method uses the waterbomb base, a common pattern for beginning many origami models.

1

Begin with the colored side face up. Fold in half.

2

Fold up.

3

Turn over.

4

Fold up.

5

Unfold everything.

6

Fold in half.

7

Fold in half and repeat behind.

8

Unfold everything.

9

Fold in half again.

10

B   A   C

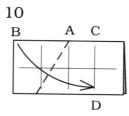

D

Using A as a guide,
fold B to the line
C–D, close to D.

11

Fold in half.

12

Turn over.

13 A   B

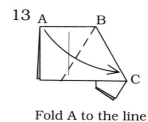

C

Fold A to the line
B–C, close to C.

14

Fold in half.

15

Unfold everything.

16

Turn over.

17

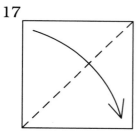

Fold diagonally in half.

18

Unfold.

19

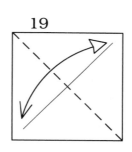

Fold and unfold.

20 A   C

E   F

B   G   D

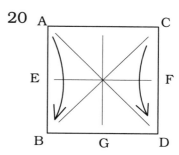

Collapse the paper on the
creases shown. A will go to
B, C to D, and E and F to G.

21

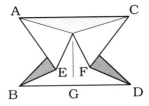

This is a three-dimensional intermediate step.

22

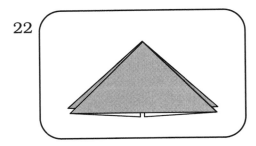

This is the Waterbomb Base.

23

Reverse-fold on the existing crease. To do this, place your finger all the way inside the model and push the dark region.

24

This is a three-dimensional intermediate step.

25

Make the same reverse fold on the three other sides. (Repeat steps 23–24 on those sides.)

29

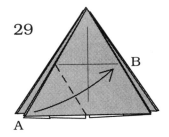

Fold A to B.

28

Fold the triangles back up but tuck them under the darker front layer. Repeat behind.

27

Fold the triangles down. Repeat behind.

26

Fold the white triangles up. Repeat behind.

30

Fold up.

31

Unfold.

32

Tuck inside the pocket.

33

Turn over.

36

Octahedron

34

Repeat steps 29–33.

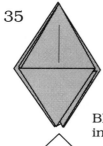

35

Blow into the bottom to inflate the octahedron.

Blue Whale

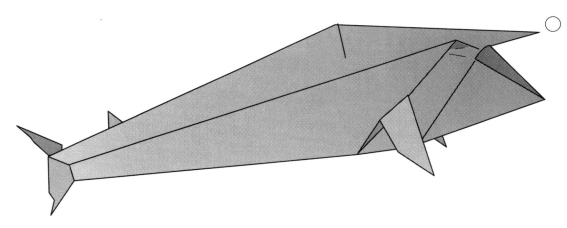

This is the largest animal in the world. The blue whale is 100 feet long and weighs over 150 tons. It spends the summers in polar waters eating over four tons of small shrimp a day. During the winter it swims towards the equator to breed.

The blue whale is a baleen whale. Baleen whales have no teeth but instead, hundreds of plates in the mouth which hang from the upper jaw. The plates, called baleen, strain out food from the water.

1

Fold and unfold along the diagonals.

2

3

4

Unfold.

5

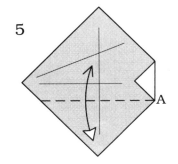

Fold up and unfold using A as a guide.

6

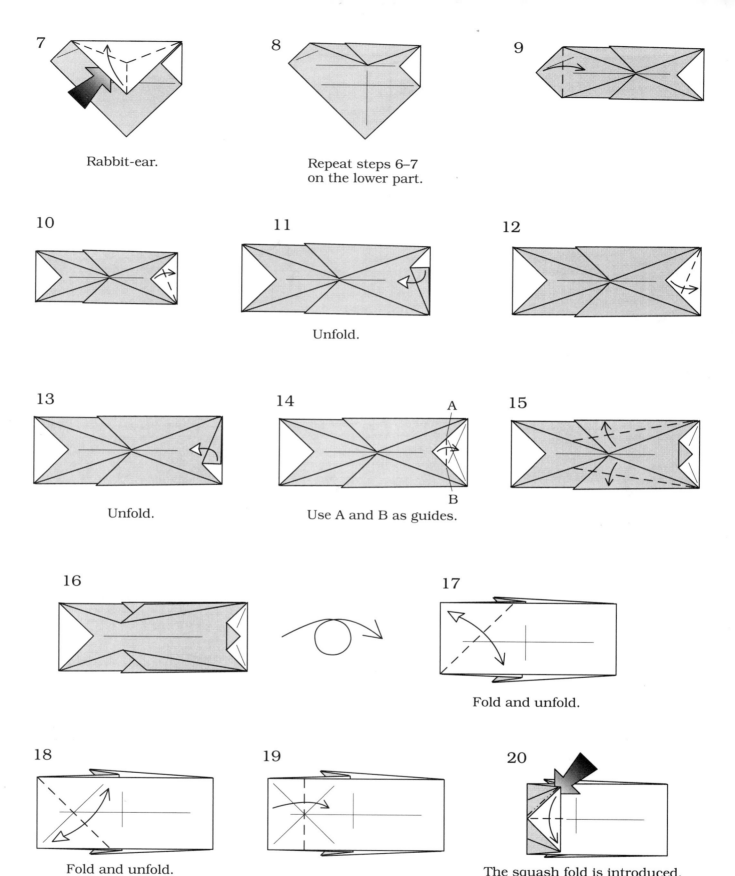

7

Rabbit-ear.

8

Repeat steps 6–7 on the lower part.

9

10

11

Unfold.

12

13

Unfold.

14

A

B

Use A and B as guides.

15

16

17

Fold and unfold.

18

Fold and unfold.

19

20

The squash fold is introduced. Place your finger as shown by the large arrow.

Blue Whale 25

21

This is a three-dimensional
intermediate step.

22

23

Unfold.

24

25

Repeat steps 20–24.

26

Unfold.

27

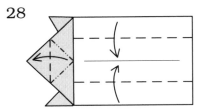

28

One form of the petal
fold is introduced.

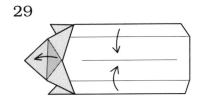

29

A three-dimensional
intermediate step.

30

A completed petal fold.
Unfold it (back to step 28).

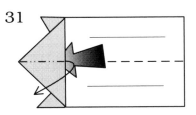

31

This is similar to a squash fold.

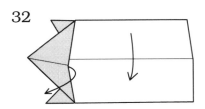

32

A three-dimensional
intermediate step.

33

Reverse-fold.

34

Reverse-fold.

35

Reverse-fold.

36

Open up.

37

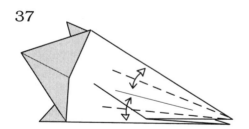

This is a three-dimensional
figure. Fold and unfold.

38

Close.

39

1. Fold the fin up.
2. Reverse-fold the tail.
Repeat behind.

40

1. Fold the fin down.
2. Make a little squash
   fold for the tail.
Repeat behind.

41

Reverse-fold the fin.
Repeat behind.

42

Form the mouth while making
the whale three-dimensional.

43

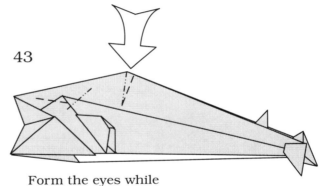

Form the eyes while
folding the mouth down.

44

Blue Whale

Narwhal

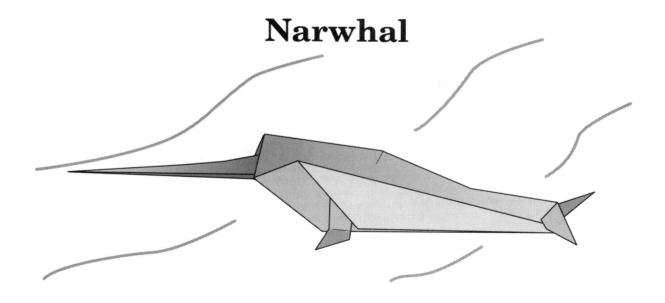

About sixteen feet long, this small whale is found in groups of 15–20 along the Arctic coasts and rivers north of Alaska. It has only two teeth, which grow from the tip of the upper jaw. The male narwhal's left tooth grows straight out to form the nine foot tusk. It eats crabs, shrimp, squid, and fish.

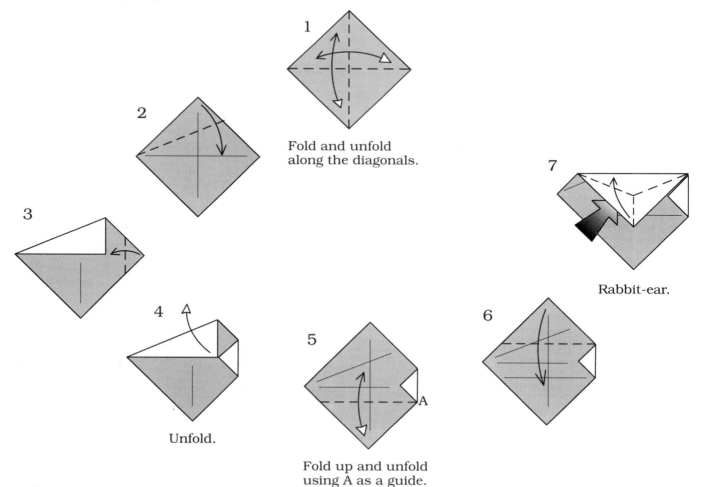

1

Fold and unfold along the diagonals.

2

3

4

Unfold.

5

Fold up and unfold using A as a guide.

6

7

Rabbit-ear.

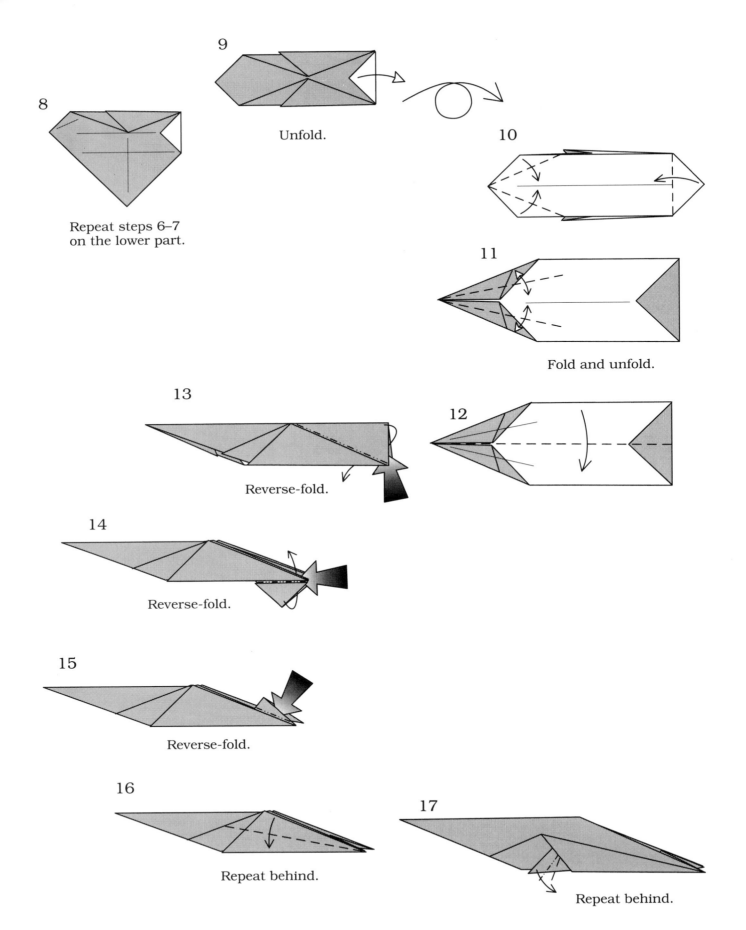

8

Repeat steps 6–7
on the lower part.

9

Unfold.

10

11

Fold and unfold.

13

Reverse-fold.

12

14

Reverse-fold.

15

Reverse-fold.

16

Repeat behind.

17

Repeat behind.

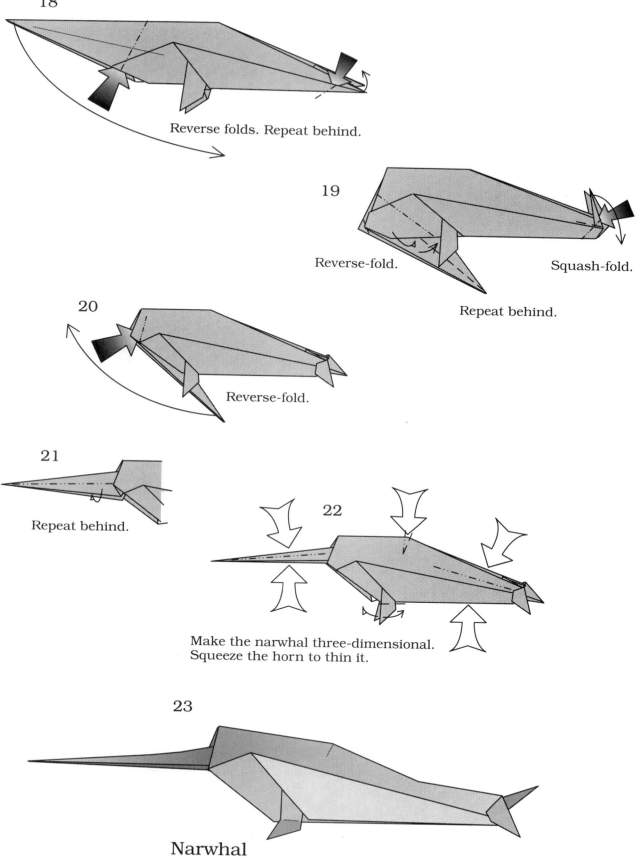

18

Reverse folds. Repeat behind.

19

Reverse-fold.

Squash-fold.

Repeat behind.

20

Reverse-fold.

21

Repeat behind.

22

Make the narwhal three-dimensional.
Squeeze the horn to thin it.

23

Narwhal

Dollar Bill

This shows how to convert a square into two rectangles which each have the proportions of a dollar bill. It can be used to fold the walrus (next model).

1

2

3

Unfold.

4

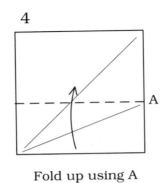

Fold up using A as a guide.

5

6

Unfold.

7

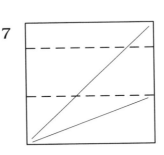

Cut along the dotted lines. The two larger rectangles have the proportions of a dollar bill.

8

Dollar Bills

Walrus

This mammal lives on ice floes in the North Altantic, North Pacific and Arctic Oceans. It is about eleven feet long and weighs 3000 pounds. With its tusks, it can dig up mollusks, crustaceans, and fish to eat.

These social animals spend much of their time resting and sleeping in the sun. They hate to be disturbed while sleeping. A walrus that is hit accidentally by another one's flipper will make a sound and hit another walrus. Then all would hit each other until they finally go back to sleep.

1

Begin with a dollar bill. Fold and unfold.

2

3

4

5

Unfold.

6

7

Reverse-fold.

8

Reverse-fold.

9

Repeat steps 5–8.

10

Rabbit ears to
form the tusks.

11

Rabbit-ear.

12

13

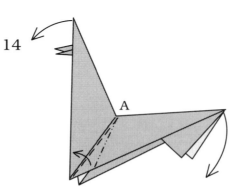

14

The outside crimp fold is
introduced. A crimp fold is
symmetric with respect to the
front and back. Pivot around A.

15

Repeat behind.

16

Tuck inside. Repeat behind.

17

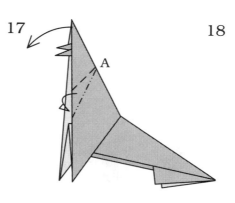

The inside crimp fold is introduced. Pivot about A.

18

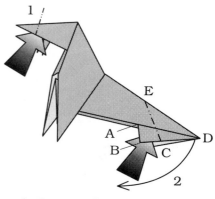

1. Reverse-fold the tip inside.
2. Reverse-fold so that
   a. Line C–D touches B and
   b. Line E–D meets A.

19

Squash-fold. Repeat behind.

20

Reverse-fold the tip and tuck it inside to lock it.

21

22

Walrus

Goose

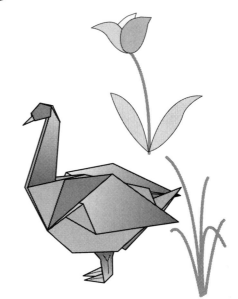

About two to three feet tall, these web-footed birds are closely related to the duck and swan. They migrate north in summer and south in winter, often flying in a line or V formation while honking energetically. Large flocks are found in grassy marshes and in grain fields. Geese eat grasses, seeds, and aquatic plants.

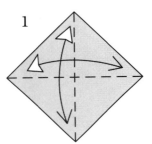

1

Fold and unfold along the diagonals.

2

Fold and unfold.

3

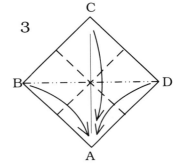

Collapse along the creases so that corners B, C, and D lie on top of A.

4

This is the Preliminary Fold. Kite-fold.

5

6

Unfold.

The folding and unfolding in steps 4–6 prepare for the petal fold. While doing the petal fold (steps 7–10) only fold upon the creases formed from steps 4–5.

7

Begin the petal fold.

8

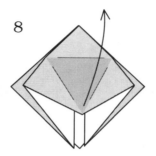

A three-dimensional
intermediate step.

9

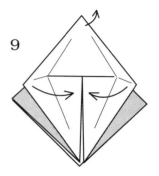

A three-dimensional
intermediate step.

10

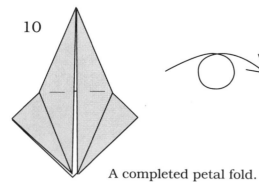

A completed petal fold.

11

12

13

Unfold.

14

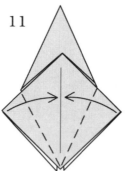

Petal-fold (repeat steps 7–10).

15

The Bird Base.

16

17

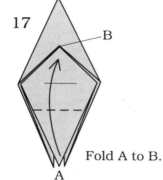

Fold A to B.

18

Unfold.

19

Fold A to C.

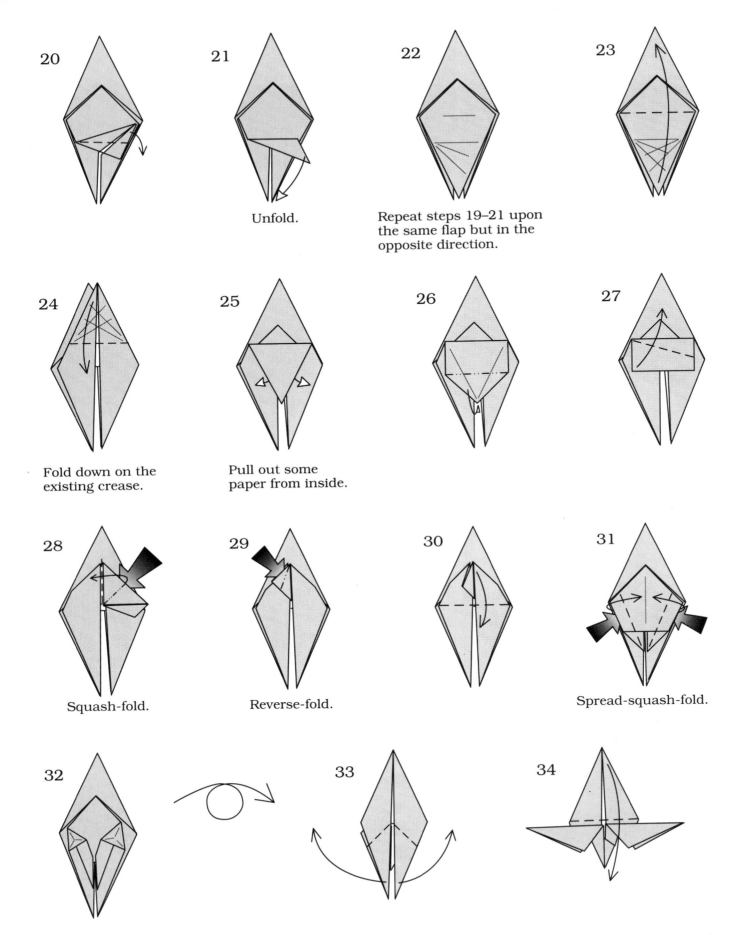

20

21

Unfold.

22

Repeat steps 19–21 upon
the same flap but in the
opposite direction.

23

24

Fold down on the
existing crease.

25

Pull out some
paper from inside.

26

27

28

Squash-fold.

29

Reverse-fold.

30

31

Spread-squash-fold.

32

33

34

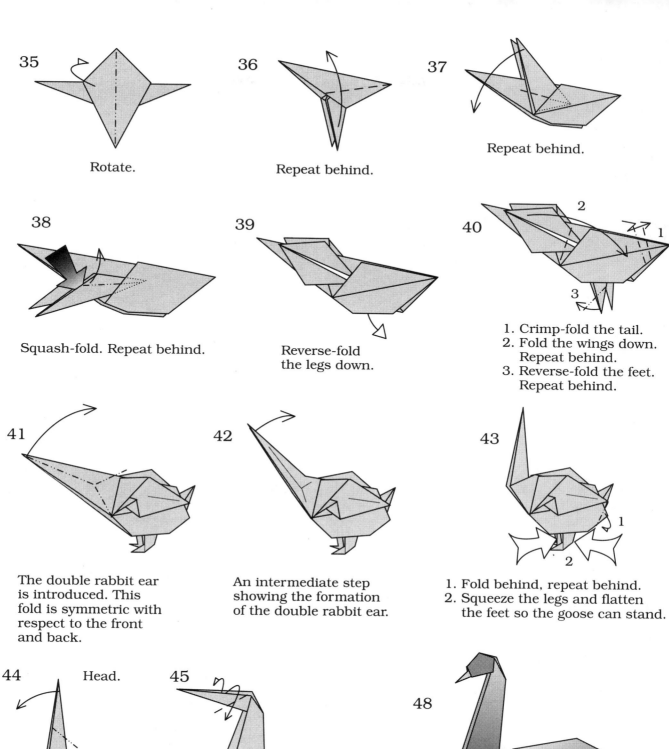

35 Rotate.

36 Repeat behind.

37 Repeat behind.

38 Squash-fold. Repeat behind.

39 Reverse-fold the legs down.

40
1. Crimp-fold the tail.
2. Fold the wings down. Repeat behind.
3. Reverse-fold the feet. Repeat behind.

41 The double rabbit ear is introduced. This fold is symmetric with respect to the front and back.

42 An intermediate step showing the formation of the double rabbit ear.

43
1. Fold behind, repeat behind.
2. Squeeze the legs and flatten the feet so the goose can stand.

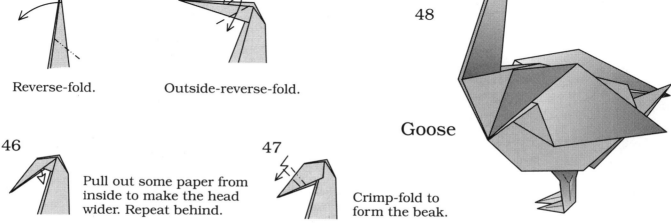

44 Head. Reverse-fold.

45 Outside-reverse-fold.

46 Pull out some paper from inside to make the head wider. Repeat behind.

47 Crimp-fold to form the beak.

48 Goose

Rooster

This is the adult male chicken. Roosters developed from the wild red jungle fowl of India and have been domesticated for 5000 years. Roosters had been used for fighting and show.

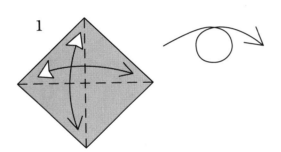

1 Fold and unfold along the diagonals.

2 Fold and unfold.

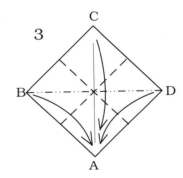

3 Collapse along the creases so that corners B, C, and D lie on top of A.

4 This is the Preliminary Fold. Fold one layer up.

5 Fold in half and unfold.

6 Fold in half and unfold.

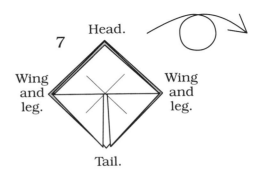

7

Head.

Wing and leg.

Wing and leg.

Tail.

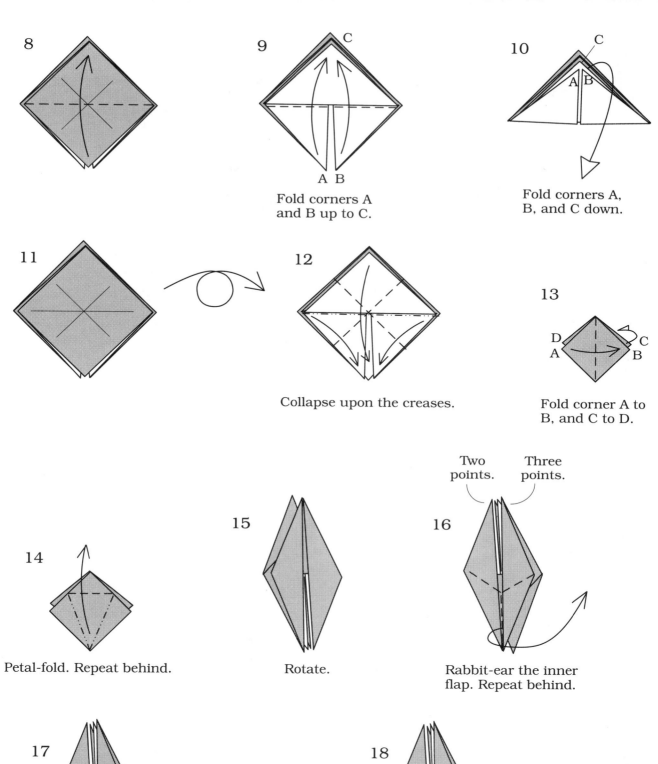

8

9

C

A B

Fold corners A
and B up to C.

10

C

A B

Fold corners A,
B, and C down.

11

12

Collapse upon the creases.

13

D   C
A   B

Fold corner A to
B, and C to D.

14

Petal-fold. Repeat behind.

15

Rotate.

Two   Three
points.   points.

16

Rabbit-ear the inner
flap. Repeat behind.

17

Pull out some paper to
make the wings wider.
Repeat behind.

18

Rabbit-ear to form the
legs. Repeat behind.

19

1. Rabbit-ear the legs to thin them.
2. Reverse-fold the tail.

20

1. Pull out the crown.
2. Fold paper from the tail inside-out.

21

Unfold the two middle tail feathers.

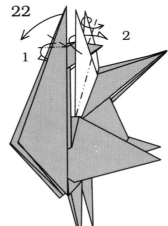

22

1. Crimp-fold the head.
2. Fold the tail feathers at two different angles.

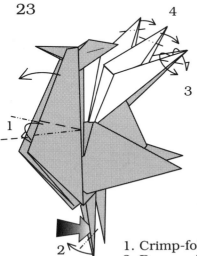

23

1. Crimp-fold the neck.
2. Reverse-fold the feet.
3. Outside-reverse-fold the lower tail feather and
4. Inside-reverse-fold the other ones.

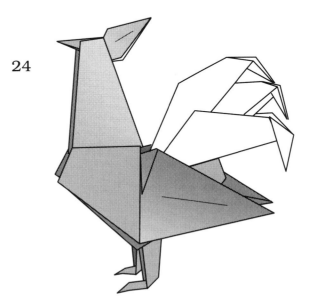

24

Rooster

Montroll's Dog Base

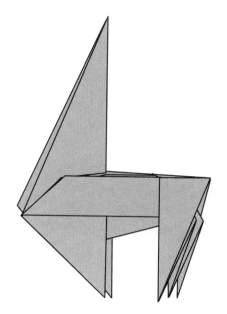

From this base, many four-legged animals can be folded which are larger in comparison to other folding methods. They are not thick, they hold together well, have impressive head detail, are well proportioned, and have a three dimensional sculptural effect. Several animals in this book use this base and variations of it.

1

2

Repeat behind.

3

Unfold, repeat behind.

4

Fold and unfold.

5

Unfold.

6

Fold and unfold.

7

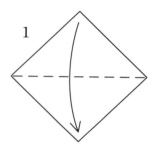

Use A as a guide.

8

9

Fold and unfold.

10

Squash-fold.

11

12

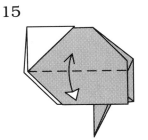

Squash-fold along the crease line so that A meets C and B falls along the line D–C. Repeat behind.

13

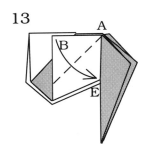

Fold B to E. Repeat behind.

14

Repeat behind.

15

Fold up and unfold. Repeat behind.

16

Fold corner A down to the line B–C and unfold.

The Dachshund uses a stretched form of Montroll's Base.

17

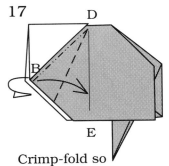

Crimp-fold so that corner B lies on the line D–E.

18

Fold the top down and unfold.

19

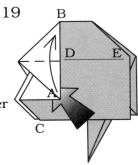

Fold A up to B. Note that corner C will lie along the line D–E. Repeat behind.

20

Squash-fold using the crease formed in step 15.

21

Fold corner G to H. The dark region will go behind the checkered area. Repeat behind.

22

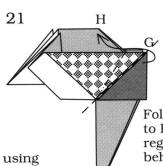

Repeat behind.

23

Using A and B as guides, pull down by unlocking some paper from behind the checkered regions. Repeat behind.

24

Place the darker grey paper on top. No valley or mountain folds are required for this step.

25

Fold the part that sticks down a little bit up. Repeat behind.

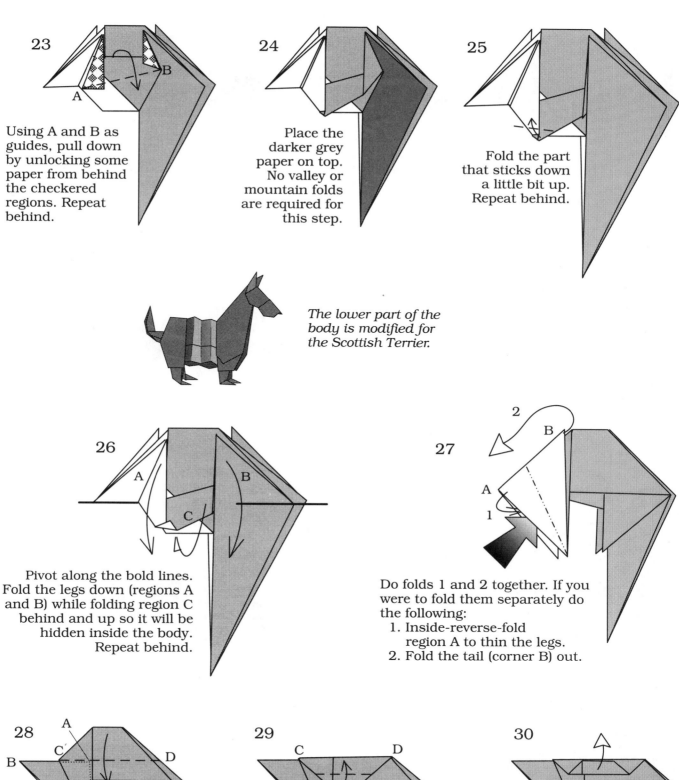

The lower part of the body is modified for the Scottish Terrier.

26

Pivot along the bold lines. Fold the legs down (regions A and B) while folding region C behind and up so it will be hidden inside the body. Repeat behind.

27

Do folds 1 and 2 together. If you were to fold them separately do the following:
  1. Inside-reverse-fold region A to thin the legs.
  2. Fold the tail (corner B) out.

28

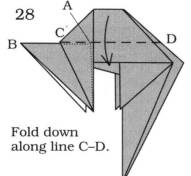

Fold down along line C–D.

29

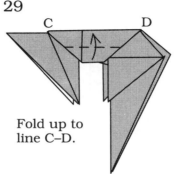

Fold up to line C–D.

30

Unfold.

The Bison and Camel have a different back formation.

31

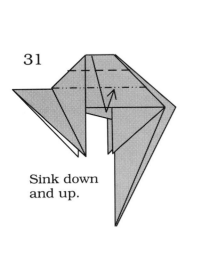

Sink down
and up.

32

Reverse-fold
the head up.

33

Reverse-fold the tail down.

34

Reverse-fold to form
the back legs and tail.
Repeat behind.

35

Montroll's Dog Base

*The Boxer is from
Montroll's Base.*

*The Horse has a
different tail formation.*

Boxer

This medium-sized noble dog is one of the most popular working breeds. It is used in police work because it is intelligent and aggressive. It is playful and gentle, making it a good family dog. It was named because of the way it appearred to be boxing with its front paws when it would begin to fight. It is about two feet high at the shoulder and weighs 60 to 70 pounds.

Begin with Montroll's Base (page 43).

1
1. Fold A to B.
2. Reverse-fold.

2
1. Unfold.
2. Crimp-fold the tail.

3
1. Reverse-fold using C and D as guides.
2. Repeat behind.
3. Outside-reverse-fold to blunt the tail.

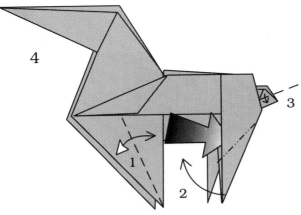

4

1. Fold in half and unfold.
   Repeat behind.
2. Reverse-fold, repeat behind.
3. Fold the tail in half to
   thin it. Repeat behind.

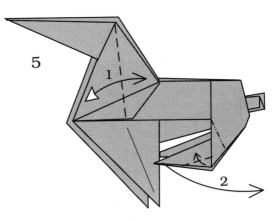

5

1. Fold and unfold.
   Repeat behind.
2. Shape the hind leg.
   Repeat behind.

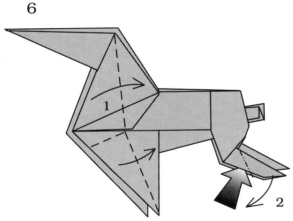

6

1. Fold the front leg and neck
   in half. Repeat behind.
2. Reverse-fold the hind leg.
   Repeat behind.

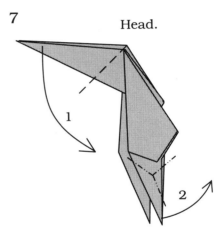

7   Head.

1. Fold down.
2. Double-rabbit-ear the
   front leg. Repeat behind.

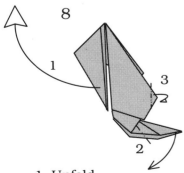

8

1. Unfold.
2. Reverse-fold. Repeat behind.
3. Mountain-fold. Repeat behind.

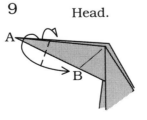

9   Head.

Outside-reverse-
fold A to B.

10

Pull out some paper.
Repeat behind.

11

Outside-reverse-fold the head.

12

Outside-reverse-fold back and forth.

13

Crimp-fold.

14

Outside-reverse-fold.

15

Crimp-fold to form the ears.

16

Fold all the feet with outside-reverse-folds.

17

1. Slide the tip of the face up.
2. Shape the ear. Repeat behind.
3. Make the top of the back three-dimensional.
4. Make the underside three-dimensional.

18

Boxer

Scottish Terrier

Also called a scottie, this dog is considered to be the oldest of the Highland terriers. Less than one foot high at the shoulder, this long haired dog is powerful and agile. It weighs about 20 pounds.

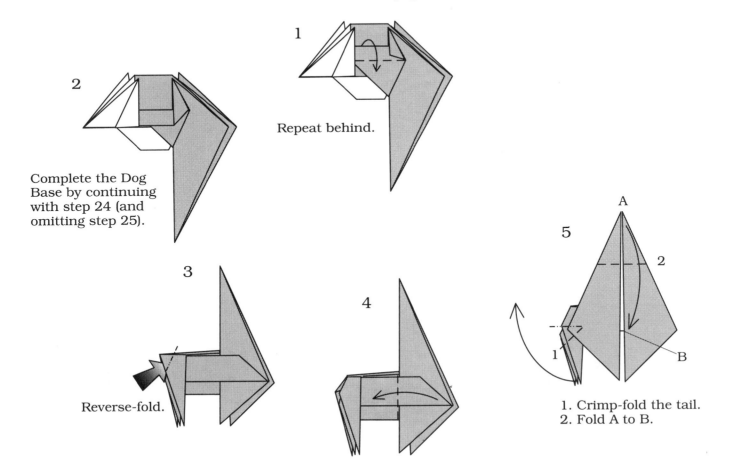

Begin with step 23 of Montroll's Base (page 43).

1

Repeat behind.

2

Complete the Dog Base by continuing with step 24 (and omitting step 25).

3

Reverse-fold.

4

5

A

2

1

B

1. Crimp-fold the tail.
2. Fold A to B.

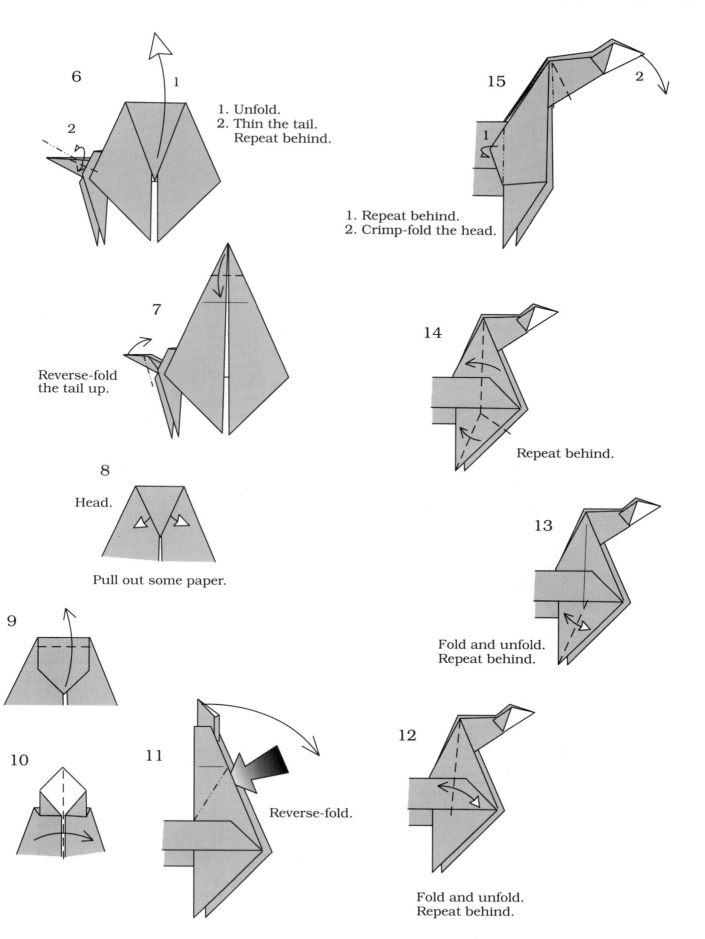

6

1. Unfold.
2. Thin the tail.
Repeat behind.

7

Reverse-fold
the tail up.

8

Head.

Pull out some paper.

9

10

11

Reverse-fold.

12

Fold and unfold.
Repeat behind.

13

Fold and unfold.
Repeat behind.

14

Repeat behind.

15

1. Repeat behind.
2. Crimp-fold the head.

16

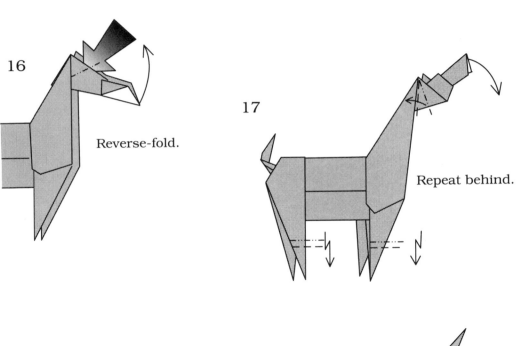

Reverse-fold.

17

Repeat behind.

18

1. Crimp-fold
2. Reverse-fold.
Repeat behind.

22

Scottish Terrier

19

Fold the darker grey paper
inside-out. Repeat behind.

21

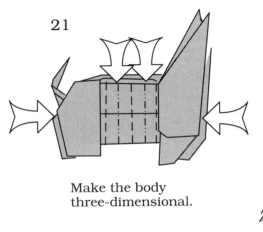

Make the body
three-dimensional.

20

Crimp and
reverse-fold.

Dachshund

This is one of the most popular pets because it is obedient, faithful, and intelligent. It is also a good sporting dog, used for hunting animals that live below the ground. This long bodied lively dog with short legs and long ears is usually reddish brown or black and tan. It has a shoulder height of about eight inches and weighs 12–22 pounds.

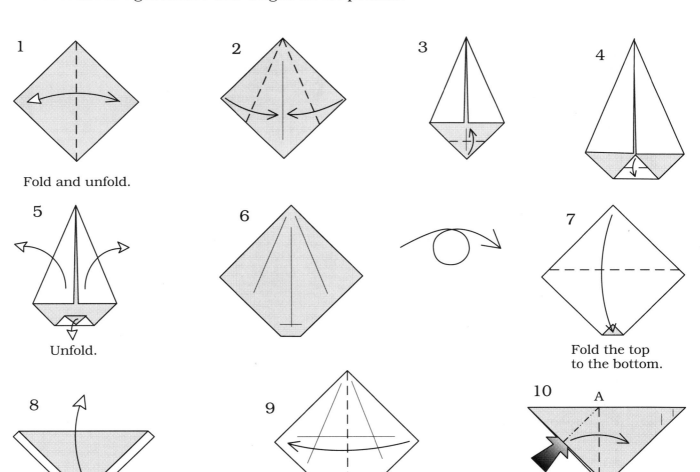

1
Fold and unfold.

2

3

4

5
Unfold.

6

7
Fold the top
to the bottom.

8
Unfold.

9
Fold in half and rotate.

10
A

B
Squash-fold along the
existing crease A–B.

11

12

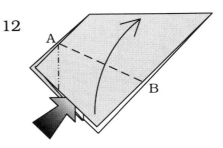

Squash-fold along the
existing crease A–B.
Repeat behind.

13

Repeat behind.

14

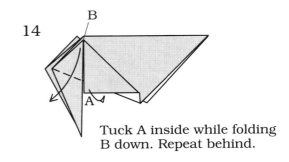

Tuck A inside while folding
B down. Repeat behind.

15

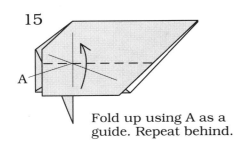

Fold up using A as a
guide. Repeat behind.

16

17

Unfold. Repeat behind.

18

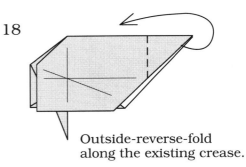

Outside-reverse-fold
along the existing crease.

19

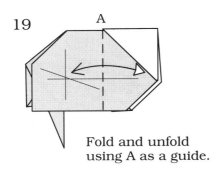

Fold and unfold
using A as a guide.

20

Continue with steps 16
through the end of
Montroll's Base (page 44).

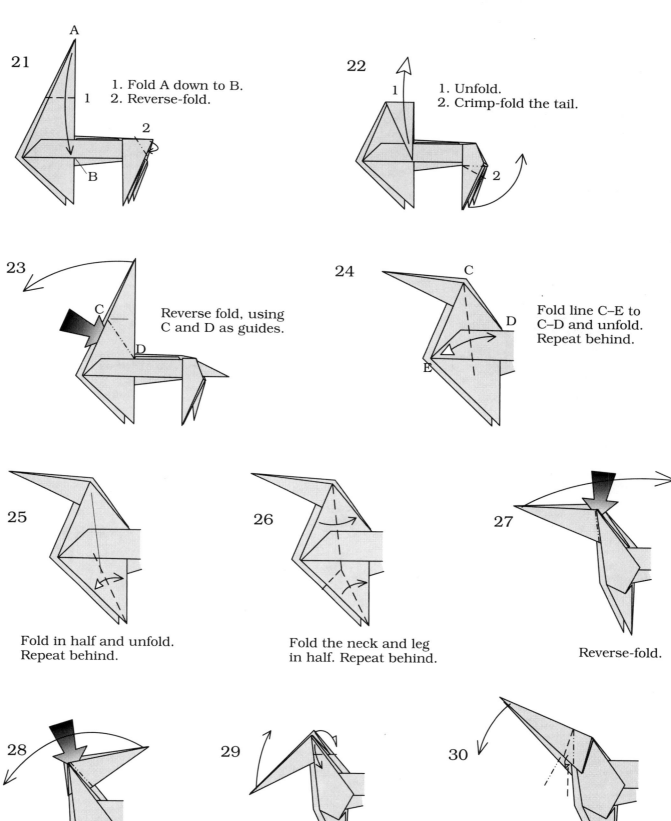

21

A

1. Fold A down to B.
2. Reverse-fold.

1

2

B

22

1

1. Unfold.
2. Crimp-fold the tail.

2

23

C

D

Reverse fold, using
C and D as guides.

24

C

D

E

Fold line C–E to
C–D and unfold.
Repeat behind.

25

Fold in half and unfold.
Repeat behind.

26

Fold the neck and leg
in half. Repeat behind.

27

Reverse-fold.

28

Reverse-fold.

29

Fold the ears down while
folding the head up.

30

Crimp-fold to form the
ears and lower the head.

31

Head.

Reverse-fold.

32

Repeat behind.

33

Front legs.

Shape the legs
with reverse folds.
Repeat behind.

34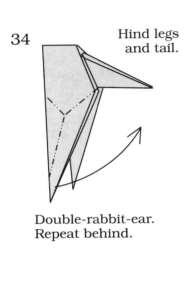

Hind legs
and tail.

Double-rabbit-ear.
Repeat behind.

35

Pleat the tail. Form the
hind legs with reverse
folds. Repeat behind.

36

Make the head, neck, and
body three-dimensional.

37

Dachshund

Husky

These mixed-breed working dogs pull sleds. They have helped on more polar journeys than any other dog. Gray or black and white, these affectionate, friendly dogs are about two feet tall at the shoulder.

The Husky uses a symmetric variation of Montroll's Base.

1

Fold and unfold.

2

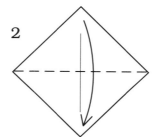

3

Fold and unfold, repeat behind.

4

Fold up and unfold creasing lightly.

5

Fold up and unfold creasing lightly.

6

Fold up and unfold creasing lightly.

7

Fold up almost to the line.

8

Fold and unfold.

9

Fold and unfold.

10

Unfold.

11

Squash-fold.

12

13

Repeat steps
11–12 on the left.

14

Squash-fold.

15

Unfold.

16

Repeat steps 14–15 on
the right and back.

17

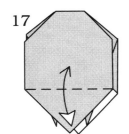

Fold up and unfold.
Repeat behind.

18

Repeat behind.

19

Fold and unfold.
Repeat behind.

20

Fold down
and unfold.

21

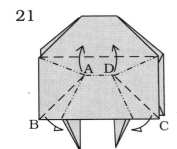

Lift A–D up while
bringing B and C
closer together.

22

23

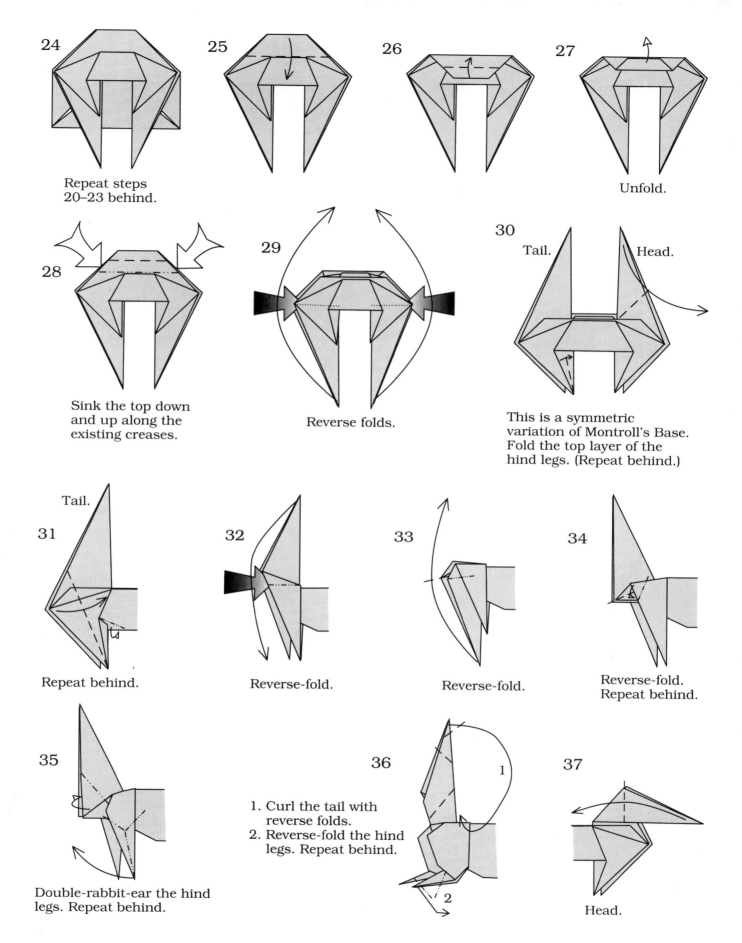

24 Repeat steps 20–23 behind.

25

26

27 Unfold.

28 Sink the top down and up along the existing creases.

29 Reverse folds.

30 Tail. Head. This is a symmetric variation of Montroll's Base. Fold the top layer of the hind legs. (Repeat behind.)

31 Tail. Repeat behind.

32 Reverse-fold.

33 Reverse-fold.

34 Reverse-fold. Repeat behind.

35 Double-rabbit-ear the hind legs. Repeat behind.

36
1. Curl the tail with reverse folds.
2. Reverse-fold the hind legs. Repeat behind.

37 Head.

38

Unfold.

39

Reverse-fold.

40

Fold and unfold.
Repeat behind.

41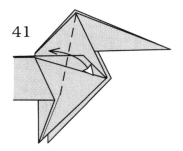

Fold and unfold.
Repeat behind.

42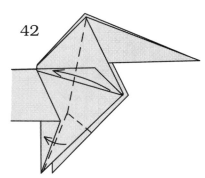

Fold the neck and leg in
half. Repeat behind.

43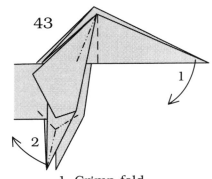

1. Crimp-fold.
2. Double-rabbit-ear.
   Repeat behind.

44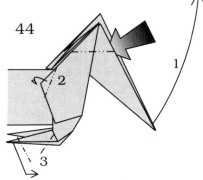

1. Reverse-fold.
2. Repeat behind.
3. Reverse folds.
   Repeat behind.

45

46

1. Reverse folds.
2. Fold the darker
   paper inside-out.
   Repeat behind.

47

Shape the head.
Repeat behind.

48

Husky

Penguin

This flightless, aquatic bird lives along the coastlines in the southern hemisphere. It is very well adapted to the cold and is an extremely fast swimmer. On land, it can run, hop, or slide on its belly. The adult is from one to four feet tall and weighs from 4 to 90 pounds. Underwater, it eats fish, shrimp, and shellfish. It spends most of its time at sea and only goes on land to breed and molt.

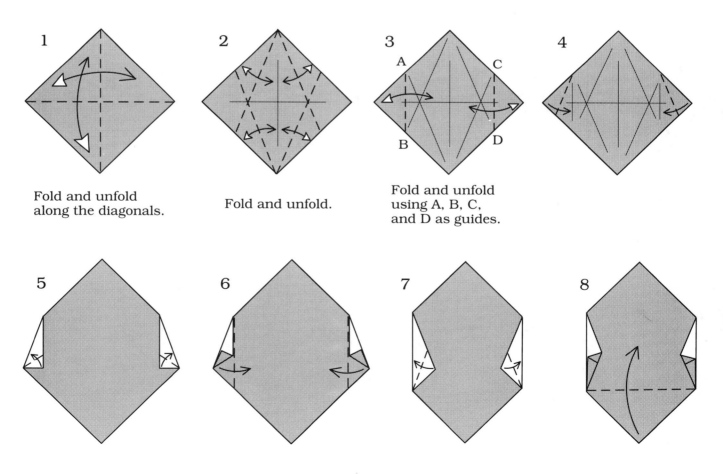

1 Fold and unfold along the diagonals.

2 Fold and unfold.

3 Fold and unfold using A, B, C, and D as guides.

4

5

6

7

8

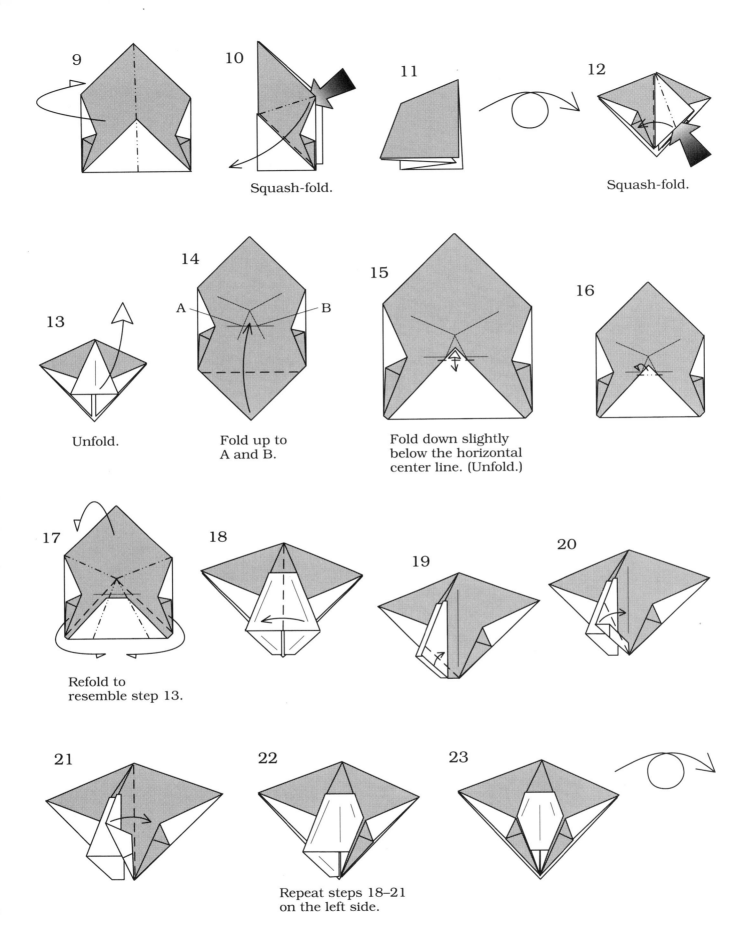

9

10

Squash-fold.

11

12

Squash-fold.

13

Unfold.

14

A   B

Fold up to
A and B.

15

Fold down slightly
below the horizontal
center line. (Unfold.)

16

17

Refold to
resemble step 13.

18

19

20

21

22

Repeat steps 18–21
on the left side.

23

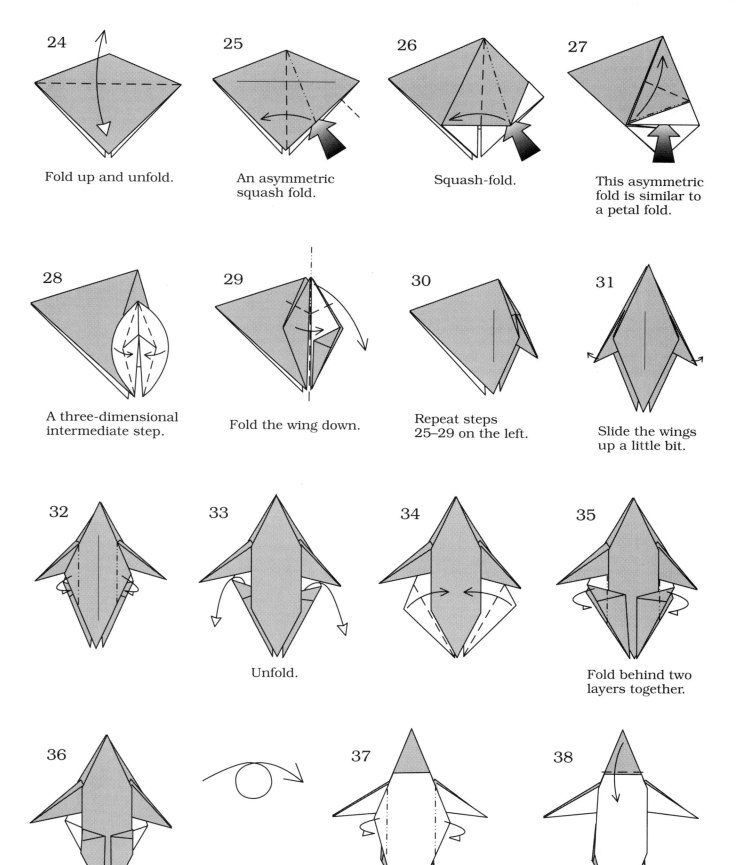

24

Fold up and unfold.

25

An asymmetric
squash fold.

26

Squash-fold.

27

This asymmetric
fold is similar to
a petal fold.

28

A three-dimensional
intermediate step.

29

Fold the wing down.

30

Repeat steps
25–29 on the left.

31

Slide the wings
up a little bit.

32

33

Unfold.

34

35

Fold behind two
layers together.

36

37

38

39

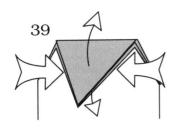

Form a three-dimensional head.

40

Two views of the head showing the formation of the beak.

41

42

43

Rabbit-ear to form the tail.

44

Reverse-fold to form the feet so they will be black on both sides.

45

Feet.

Squash folds.

46

47

To make the penguin three-dimensional place one finger inside and with your other hand, squeeze near the neck to puff out the body.

48

Penguin

Peacock

The peacock, which is the male peafowl, has a large green or blue body plumage and head crests. In full plumage it is about seven feet tall. The plumes, which are long feathers, are not the tail. It lives by river banks, forest clearings, or other places with scattered trees. It flies quite well and travels in small flocks. The peacock feeds on seeds and grasses.

1

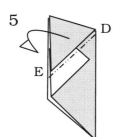

Fold and unfold
along the diagonals.

2

Fold two corners
to the center.

3

4

A

B

C

Bring A down
to the line B–C.

5

D

E

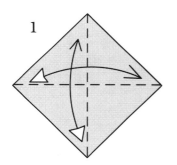

Fold behind
along D–E.

6

Squash-fold and rotate.

7

8

Unfold.

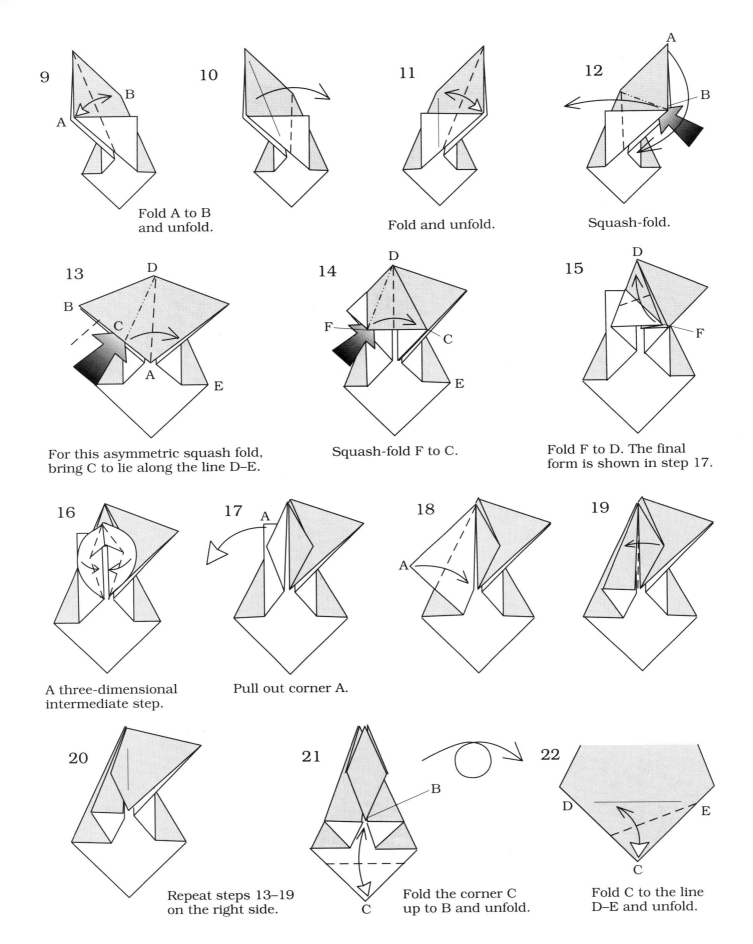

9

B

A

Fold A to B
and unfold.

10

Fold and unfold.

11

12

A

B

Squash-fold.

13

D

B

C

A

E

For this asymmetric squash fold,
bring C to lie along the line D–E.

14

D

F

C

E

Squash-fold F to C.

15

D

F

Fold F to D. The final
form is shown in step 17.

16

A three-dimensional
intermediate step.

17

A

Pull out corner A.

18

A

19

20

Repeat steps 13–19
on the right side.

21

B

C

Fold the corner C
up to B and unfold.

22

D

E

C

Fold C to the line
D–E and unfold.

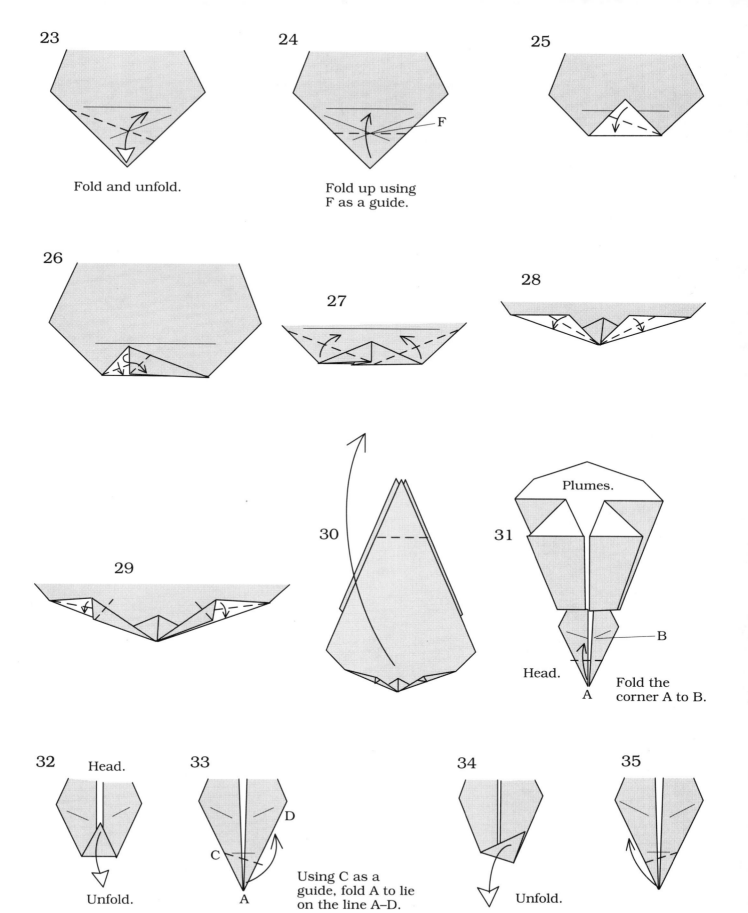

23

Fold and unfold.

24

F

Fold up using
F as a guide.

25

26

27

28

29

30

31

Plumes.

Head.

A

B

Fold the
corner A to B.

32 Head.

Unfold.

33

D

C

A

Using C as a
guide, fold A to lie
on the line A–D.

34

Unfold.

35

36

Pull out some
paper along one
of the creases.

37

Squash-fold.

38

Pull out
some paper.

39

40

Squash-fold and rotate.

41

42

Slide the plumes up.

Plumes.

43

Head.

A

B

Legs and tail.

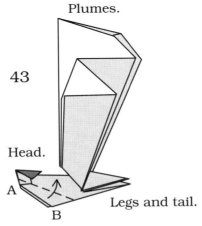

Fold A–B up so that it
is under the darker
paper. Repeat behind.

44

Outside reverse folds form
the neck. Lift up some
paper by the tail to shape
the wings. Repeat behind.

45

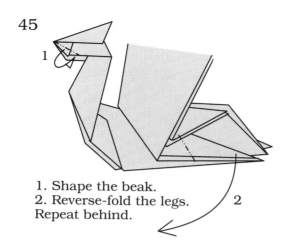

1. Shape the beak.
2. Reverse-fold the legs.
Repeat behind.

2

46

Wings will form as the tail is folded up. Pinch the tip of the head to form the beak. Make the neck three-dimensional. Repeat behind.

47

Leg.

Crimp-fold the leg. Repeat behind.

48

Plumes.

Repeat behind.

49

Repeat behind.

50

Repeat behind.

51

Repeat behind.

52

Sink. Repeat behind.

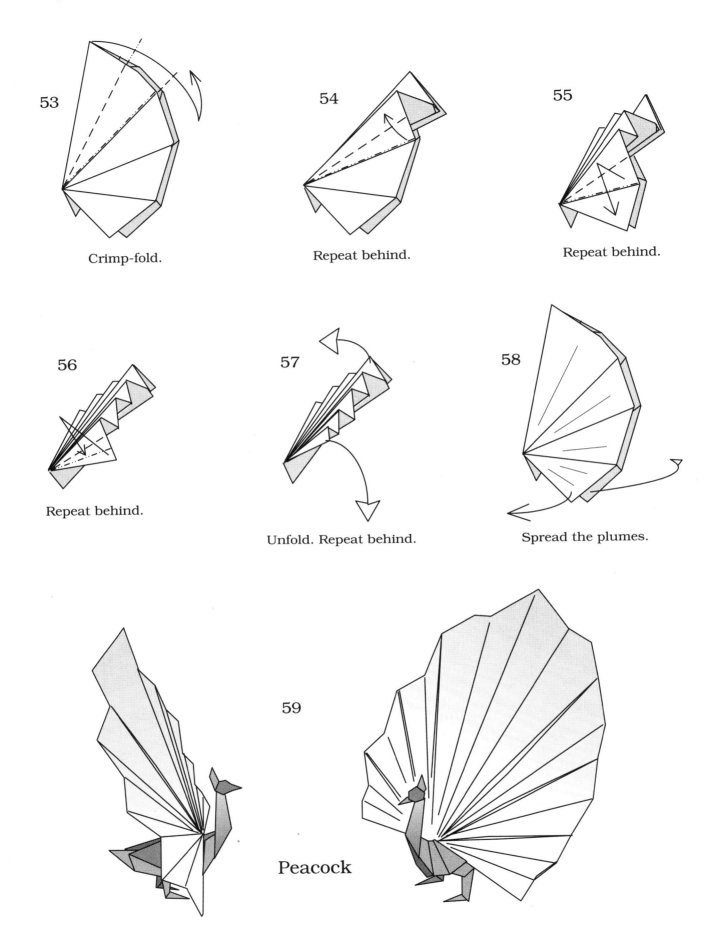

53

Crimp-fold.

54

Repeat behind.

55

Repeat behind.

56

Repeat behind.

57

Unfold. Repeat behind.

58

Spread the plumes.

59

Peacock

Horse

Horses have been associated with mankind throughout history. For thousands of years, they were hunted for food. Then they became domesticated and were used in warfare to pull chariots. Their use in warfare lasted into this century. Today they are used for riding and racing.

About six feet tall, the horse is highly adapted for fast, graceful running. It feeds on grass.

Begin with step 33 of Montroll's Base (page 43).

1

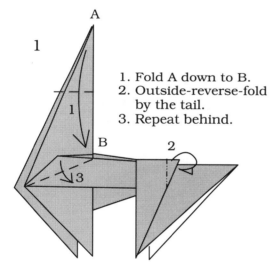

1. Fold A down to B.
2. Outside-reverse-fold by the tail.
3. Repeat behind.

2

1. Squash-fold C down to lie on the line C–D.
2. Fold behind along the line E–B.

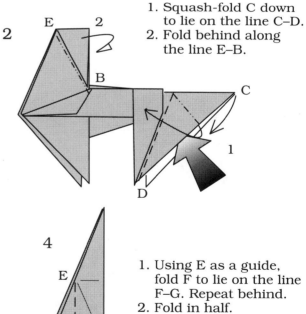

3

1. Unfold—fold A back up.
2. Kite-fold and unfold. Repeat behind.
3. Fold behind to shape the tail.

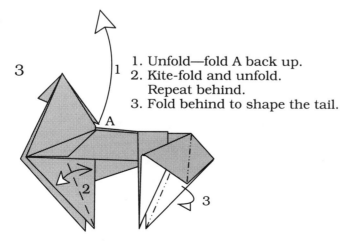

4

1. Using E as a guide, fold F to lie on the line F–G. Repeat behind.
2. Fold in half. Repeat behind.

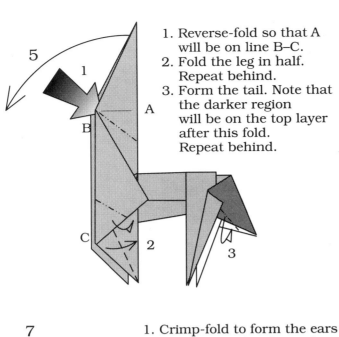

5

1. Reverse-fold so that A will be on line B–C.
2. Fold the leg in half. Repeat behind.
3. Form the tail. Note that the darker region will be on the top layer after this fold. Repeat behind.

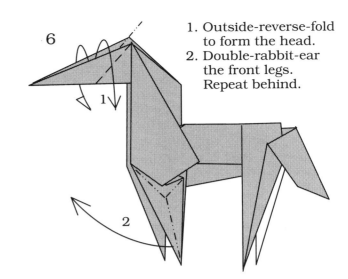

6

1. Outside-reverse-fold to form the head.
2. Double-rabbit-ear the front legs. Repeat behind.

7

1. Crimp-fold to form the ears and fold the head up a bit.
2. Fold behind, repeat behind.
3. Slide only one leg down.
4. Place the darker region above. Repeat behind.

8

1. Crimp-fold to form the mouth.
2. Crimp-fold to bend the neck.
3. Reverse-fold the front leg.
4. Double-rabbit-ear the hind leg. Repeat behind.

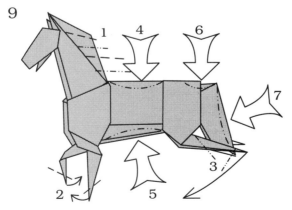

9

1. Pleat the main.
2. Form the front hooves.
3. Shape the hind legs and hooves.
4. Make the back three-dimensional.
5. Make the underside three-dimensional.
6. Shape the top of the tail.
7. Shape the tail.

10

Horse

Bison

The American bison used to live in the Great Plains of North America. Indians hunted bison for food and clothing. Today bison are mainly found in game reserves. They are about eleven feet long and six feet high at the shoulder, and they weigh about a ton. Primarily grazers, they live in herds. They have a good sense of hearing and smell.

Begin with Montroll's Base (page 43) but omit steps 28-31.

1

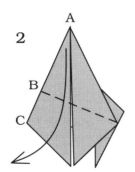

2

A

B

C

Fold down so that line A–B meets corner C.

3

4

Unfold.

5

Repeat steps 2–4 folding down toward the right side.

6

Squash-fold along the existing creases.

7

Squash-fold.

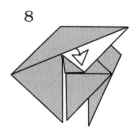

8

Pull out some paper.

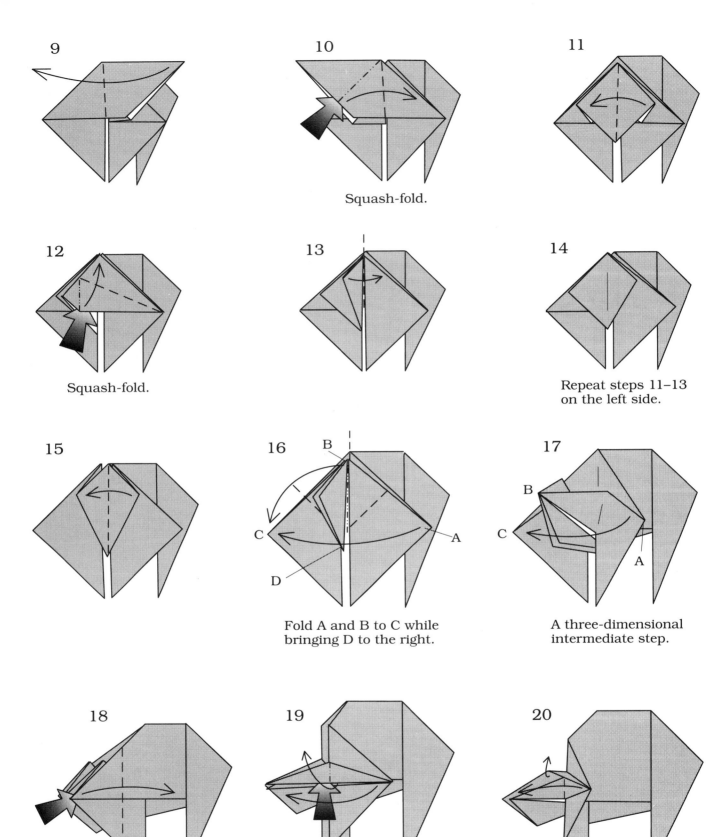

9

10

Squash-fold.

11

12

Squash-fold.

13

14

Repeat steps 11–13
on the left side.

15

16

Fold A and B to C while
bringing D to the right.

17

A three-dimensional
intermediate step.

18

Squash-fold,
repeat behind.

19

Fold one of the two layers
up. Repeat behind.

20

A three-dimensional
intermediate step.
Repeat behind.

21

Repeat behind.

22

Crimp-fold the head.

23

1. Unfold the back.
2. Pull the horn out.
   Repeat behind.

24

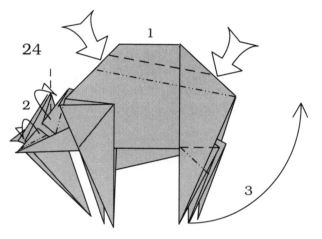

1. Sink down and up to form the back.
2. Reverse folds at the head. Repeat behind.
3. Crimp-fold the tail.

25

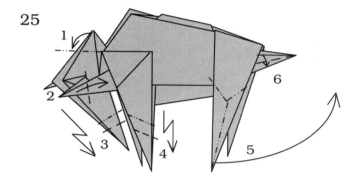

1. Reverse-fold the tip of the head inside.
2. Fold the horn to the right. Repeat behind.
3. Crimp-fold the beard.
4. Crimp-fold the front legs. Repeat behind.
5. Double-rabbit-ear the hind legs. Repeat behind.
6. Thin the tail. Repeat behind.

26

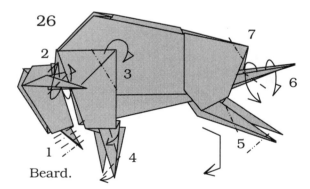

Beard.

1. Pleat the beard.
2. Outside-reverse-fold the horn up
   to make it white. Repeat behind.
3. Repeat behind.
4. Shape the front legs.
   Repeat behind for each leg.
5. Reverse folds to shape the
   hind legs. Repeat behind.
6. Outside-reverse-fold the tail.
7. Reverse-fold.

27

Bison

Camel

This is the two-humped, or Bacterian camel. It is easily tamed and moves slowly. It is seven feet high at the humps and eats salty plants, fish, animal flesh, skin, and bones. Native to the plains of Central Asia, it is well adapted to tolerate cold and snowy winters. Its long, shaggy hair keeps it warm in winter. The camel sheds its coat in the summer.

Begin with Montroll's Base (page 43) but omit steps 24-28.

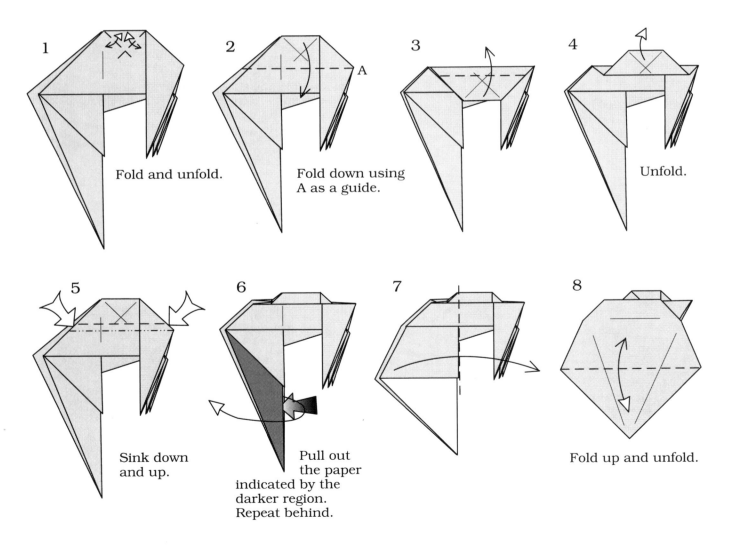

1. Fold and unfold.

2. Fold down using A as a guide.

3.

4. Unfold.

5. Sink down and up.

6. Pull out the paper indicated by the darker region. Repeat behind.

7.

8. Fold up and unfold.

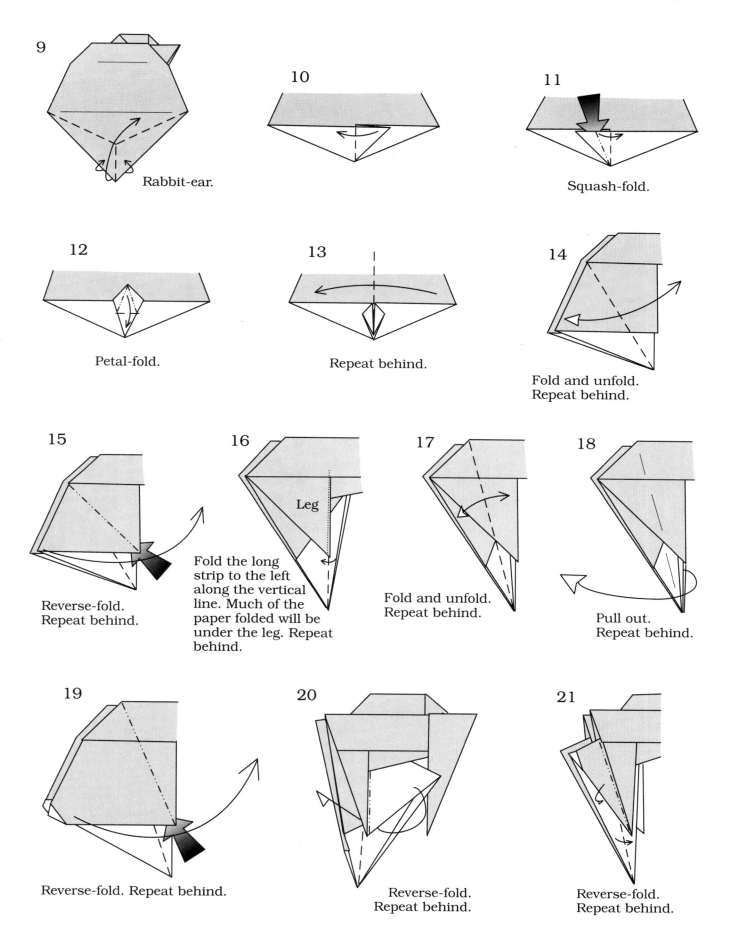

9

Rabbit-ear.

10

11

Squash-fold.

12

Petal-fold.

13

Repeat behind.

14

Fold and unfold.
Repeat behind.

15

Reverse-fold.
Repeat behind.

16

Leg

Fold the long
strip to the left
along the vertical
line. Much of the
paper folded will be
under the leg. Repeat
behind.

17

Fold and unfold.
Repeat behind.

18

Pull out.
Repeat behind.

19

Reverse-fold. Repeat behind.

20

Reverse-fold.
Repeat behind.

21

Reverse-fold.
Repeat behind.

Camel 77

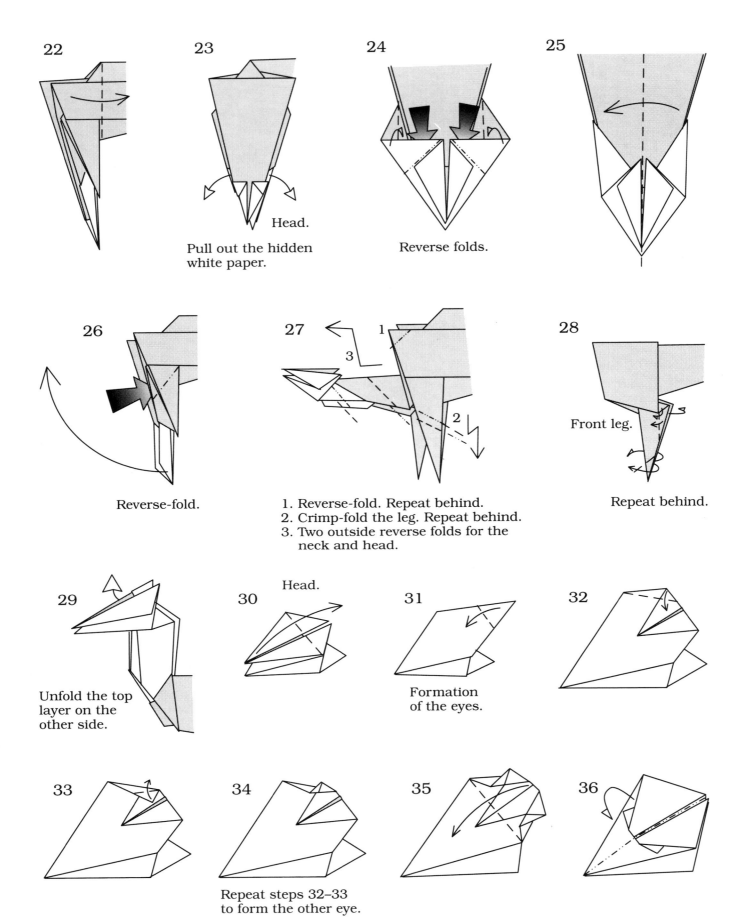

22

23

Pull out the hidden
white paper.

Head.

24

Reverse folds.

25

26

Reverse-fold.

27

1. Reverse-fold. Repeat behind.
2. Crimp-fold the leg. Repeat behind.
3. Two outside reverse folds for the
   neck and head.

28

Front leg.

Repeat behind.

29

Unfold the top
layer on the
other side.

Head.

30

31

Formation
of the eyes.

32

33

34

Repeat steps 32–33
to form the other eye.

35

36

37

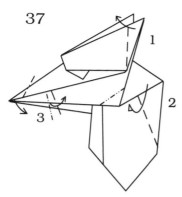

1. Fold the ear. Repeat behind.
2. Form the neck. Repeat behind.
3. Crimp-fold the mouth.

38

Reverse-fold.

39

Crimp-fold to
form the tail.

40

1. Thin the tail.
2. Double-rabbit-ear to
   form the hind leg.
Repeat behind.

41

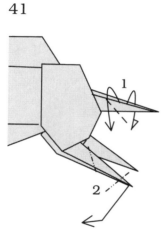

1. Outside-reverse-fold the tail.
2. Reverse folds to form the leg
   and hoof. Repeat behind.

42

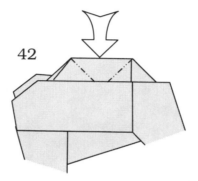

Formation of the humps.

43

This is a three-
dimensional figure.
Repeat behind.

44

Repeat behind.

45

Camel

Dromedary

The dromedary, or Arabian camel, has one hump and is completely domesticated. It is seven or eight feet tall at the shoulder and lives in the sandy regions of Western Asia, India, Arabia, and Africa. It is very well adapted to desert life. It has a double layer of protective eyelashes and can shut its nostrils during sand storms. The hump protects it from the sun by absorbing heat and carries its fat reserves. It feeds on plants and can go for three to nine days without water. It has keen eyesight and a good sense of smell.

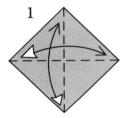

1

Fold and unfold along the diagonals.

2

Crease lightly.

3

Unfold.

4

Fold up to the center and unfold. Crease lightly and only on the left side.

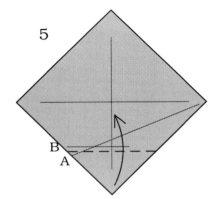

5

Fold up so that A meets the line above it, close to B.

6

Note how the creases intersect inside the circle.

7

8

9

Unfold and rotate.

10

11

12

13

Unfold.

14

15

Squash-fold.

16

17

Squash-fold.

18

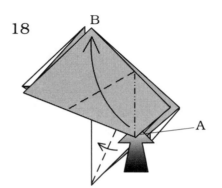

B

A

Squash-fold A up to B.
Repeat behind.

19

Unfold. Repeat behind.

20

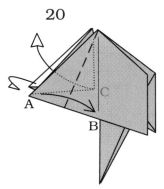

Pull out corner C while folding A to B and repeating behind.

21

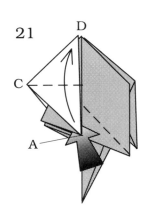

Squash-fold A up to D. Repeat behind.

22

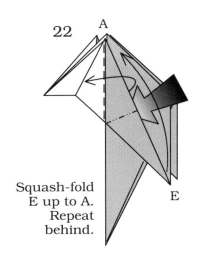

Squash-fold E up to A. Repeat behind.

23

Repeat behind.

24

Squash-fold. Repeat behind.

25

Petal-fold. Repeat behind.

26

Place the darker region on top.

27

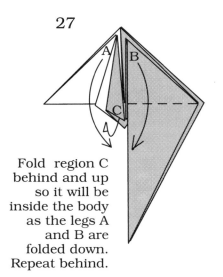

Fold region C behind and up so it will be inside the body as the legs A and B are folded down. Repeat behind.

28

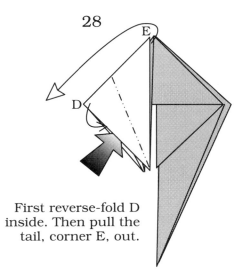

First reverse-fold D inside. Then pull the tail, corner E, out.

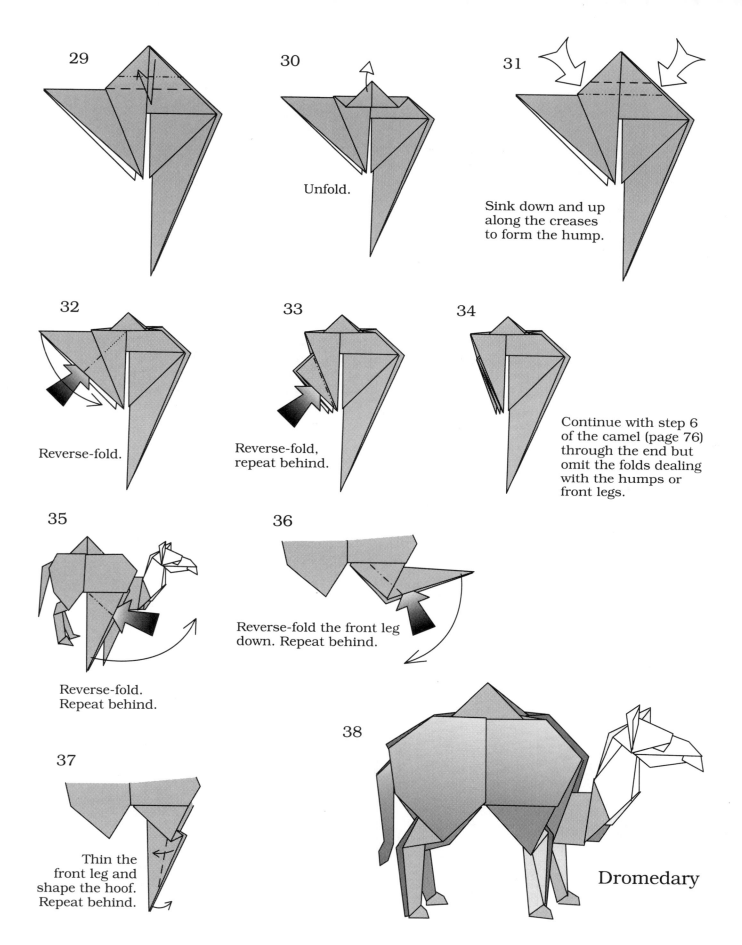

29

30

Unfold.

31

Sink down and up
along the creases
to form the hump.

32

Reverse-fold.

33

Reverse-fold,
repeat behind.

34

Continue with step 6
of the camel (page 76)
through the end but
omit the folds dealing
with the humps or
front legs.

35

Reverse-fold.
Repeat behind.

36

Reverse-fold the front leg
down. Repeat behind.

37

Thin the
front leg and
shape the hoof.
Repeat behind.

38

Dromedary

Rhinoceros

This nocturnal mammal lives in the warmer parts of Southern Asia and Africa. It has one or two horns which are made from hardened hairs. During its life, the horns continue to grow and are rubbed down from contact with trees or rocks. Rhinos are good swimmers. The rhinoceros shown here is the white rhinoceros, the largest of the rhinos, standing over six feet high at the shoulder and weighing over three tons. Its pale gray skin sometimes becomes a reddish brown from wallowing in mud. The rhino feeds on grasses and other forms of vegetation.

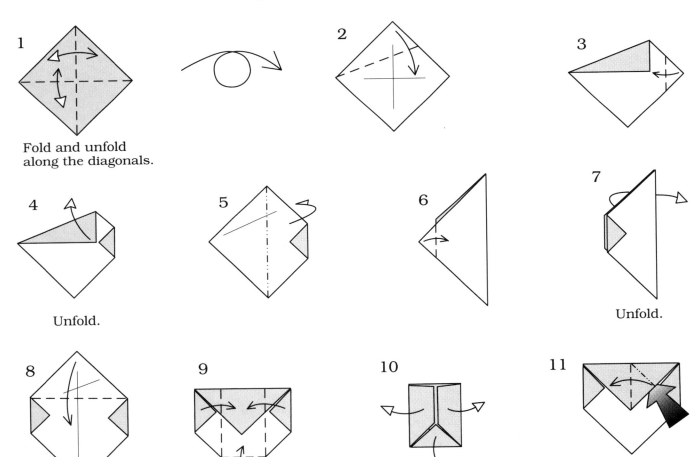

1 Fold and unfold along the diagonals.

2

3

4 Unfold.

5

6

7 Unfold.

8

9

10 Unfold.

11 Squash-fold.

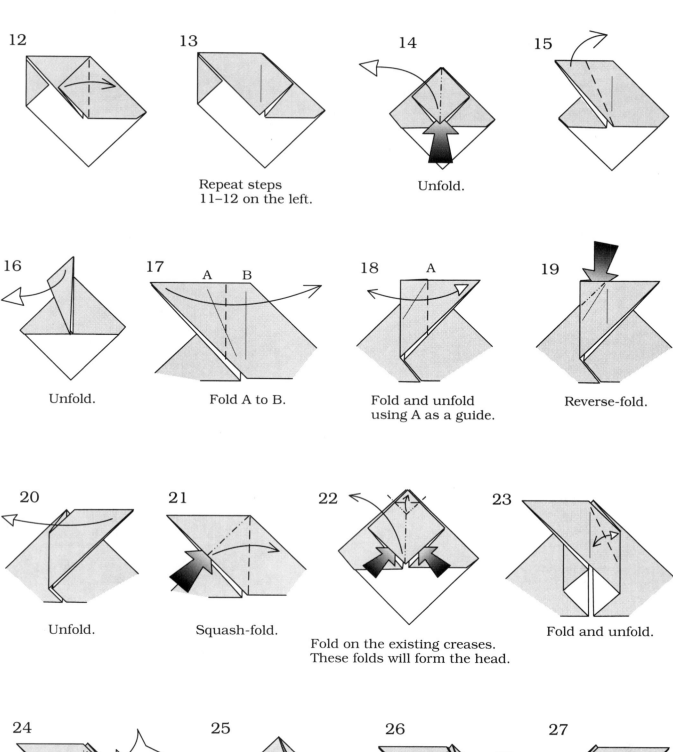

12

13

Repeat steps
11–12 on the left.

14

Unfold.

15

16

Unfold.

17

A   B

Fold A to B.

18

A

Fold and unfold
using A as a guide.

19

Reverse-fold.

20

Unfold.

21

Squash-fold.

22

Fold on the existing creases.
These folds will form the head.

23

Fold and unfold.

24

Sink.

25

This is a three-dimensional
figure showing the formation
of the sink fold.

26

27

Repeat steps
23–24 on the left.

28

Squash-fold.

29

Fold up and unfold.

30

Squash-fold.

31

32

Repeat steps
30–31 on the left.

33

Petal-fold.

34

Reverse folds.

35

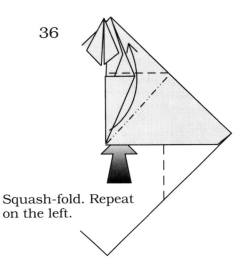

36

Squash-fold. Repeat
on the left.

37

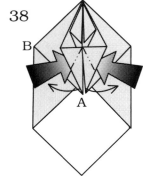

38

B

A

Reverse-fold so that A
does not quite meet B.

39

B

A

Reverse-fold.

40

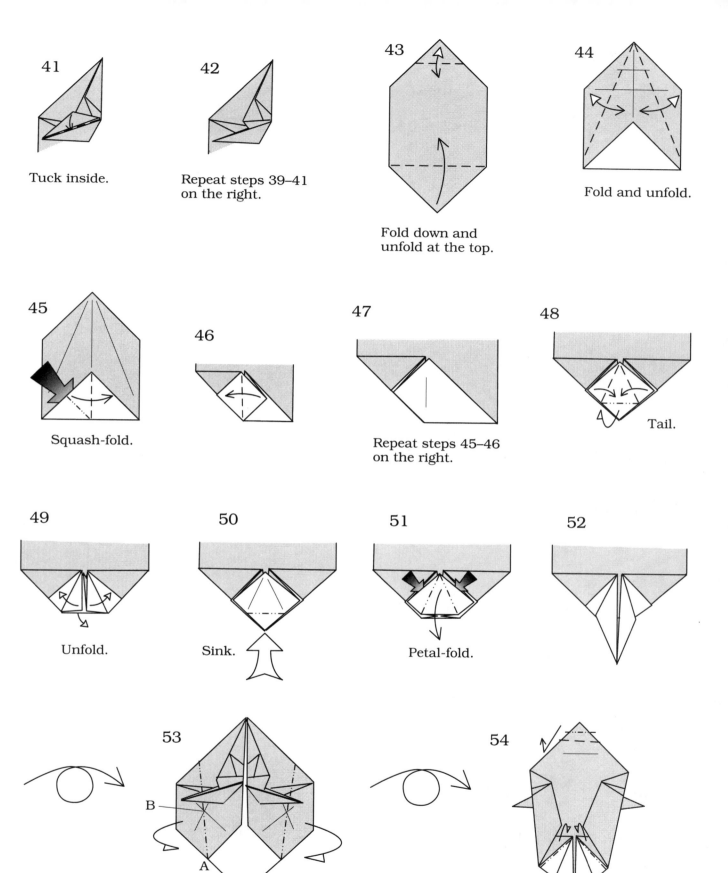

41

Tuck inside.

42

Repeat steps 39–41
on the right.

43

Fold down and
unfold at the top.

44

Fold and unfold.

45

Squash-fold.

46

47

Repeat steps 45–46
on the right.

48

Tail.

49

Unfold.

50

Sink.

51

Petal-fold.

52

53

B

A

A and B are
the guides.

54

55

56

57

Fold the white
part inside-out.

58

Head.

59

1. Rabbit-ear the horn.
2. Squash-fold the ear.

60

61

Form the other ear
(from steps 58–61).

62

Though the body is
folded in half, do not try
to fold the head in half.

63

Pull out the hind legs
while folding the tail up.

64

65

Hind legs and tail.

Fold and unfold. Note that this crease does not come to a point at the bottom.

66

Tuck inside.

67

68

69

Repeat behind.

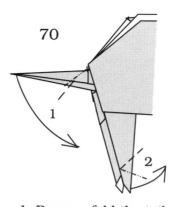

70

1. Reverse-fold the tail.
2. Squash-fold the foot. Repeat behind.

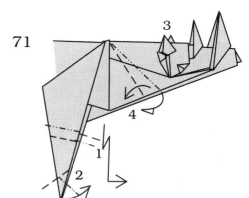

71

1. Crimp-fold the front legs. Repeat behind.
2. Squash-fold the feet. Repeat behind.
3. Open the ears. Repeat behind.
4. Crimp-fold the neck.

72

Make the rhinoceros three-dimensional.

73

Rhinoceros

Insect Base

1

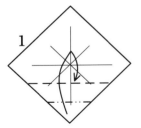

First fold and
unfold diagonally
and rectangularly.
Divide in thirds.

2

3

4

Unfold.

5

6

Unfold.

7

8

Unfold.

9

10

Repeat steps 7–9.

11

Unfold.

12

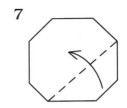

Repeat steps 7–11
in the opposite
direction.

13

14

15

Squash-fold.

16

Squash-fold.

17

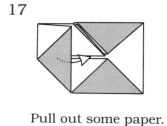

Pull out some paper.

18

Squash-fold.

19

20

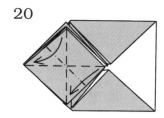

This fold is very similar
to the construction of
the waterbomb base.

21

Repeat steps 19–20 on
the upper left hand side.

22

Repeat steps 15–21
on the right.

23

24

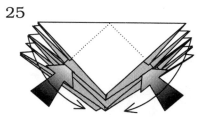

25

Reverse-fold the
center flaps down.

26

Make eight reverse
folds. (Four in front
and four behind.)

27

Unfold, repeat behind.

28

Repeat behind.

29

Repeat behind.

30

31

Repeat steps 27–28.

32

Sink the original
center of the paper.

33

Repeat behind.

34

35

Squash-fold.

36

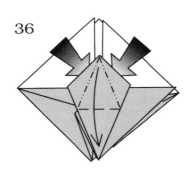

This is similar
to a petal fold.

37

38

39

Repeat steps 35–38
on the right.

40

41

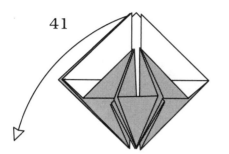

Pull out the paper.

42

43

44

Squash-fold.

45

Squash-fold.

46

47

Unfold.

48

Crimp-fold.

49

Repeat behind.

50

Reverse-fold,
repeat behind.

51

Repeat steps 41–50
on the right.

52

53

Squash-fold.

54

55

56

57

Repeat steps 53–56
on the right.

58

Pull A and B up.

59

A three-dimensional figure.

60

Fold and unfold.

61

62

63

Crimp-fold.

64

65

Remember when the
center was sunk (in step
32)? Sink this little
triangular flap inside the
sunken center.

66

67

Reverse-fold.

68

Repeat steps 60–67
on the right.

69

Insect Base

Weevil

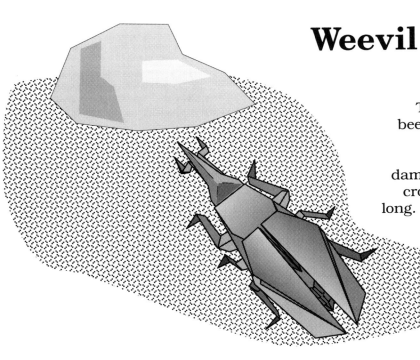

The weevil is a member of the snout beetle family. It has a hard body and a long head pointing downward. This insect is a pest which does much damage to grain, cotton, nut, and other crops. It is about 1/16 to 1/2 an inch long. Most are gray, black, or brown, but some are bright blue and green.

Begin with the Insect Base (page 90).

1

Unfold.

2

Unfold.

3

Reverse-fold.

4

Reverse-fold.

5

Reverse-fold.

6

Spread-squash-fold.

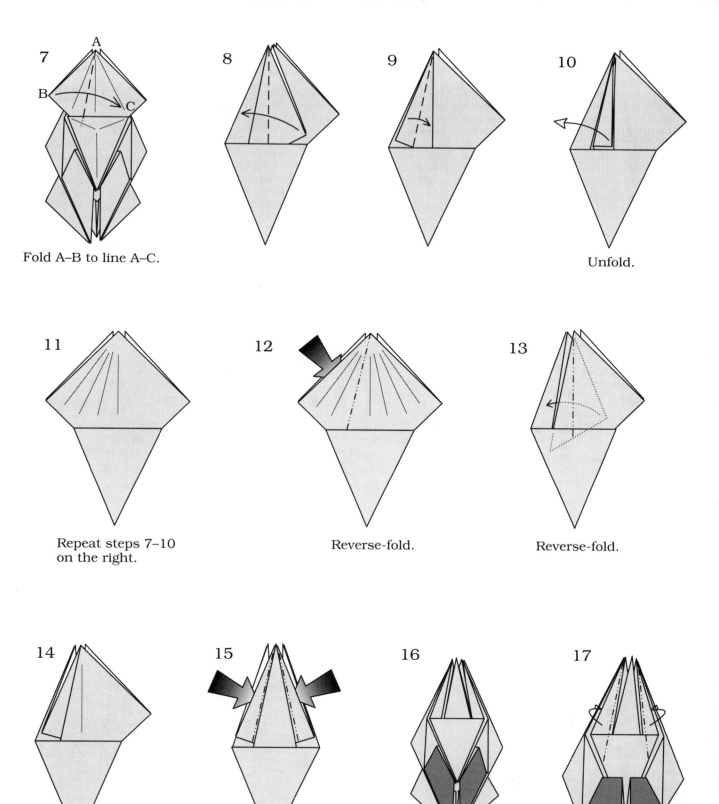

7 Fold A–B to line A–C.

8

9

10 Unfold.

11 Repeat steps 7–10 on the right.

12 Reverse-fold.

13 Reverse-fold.

14 Repeat steps 12–13 on the right.

15 Reverse folds.

16 Place the darker grey paper above.

17

18

19

20

21

Reverse folds.

22

23

24

Reverse folds.

Squash folds.

Reverse folds.

25

26

27

Reverse folds.

Reverse folds, repeat behind.

Double-rabbit-ear the two front legs.

28

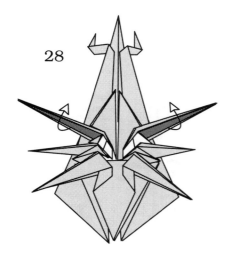

Pull out the top layers, repeat behind.

29

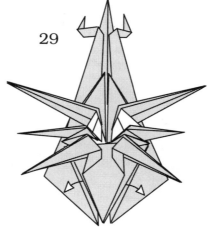

Pull out some paper.

30

Shape the tail.

31

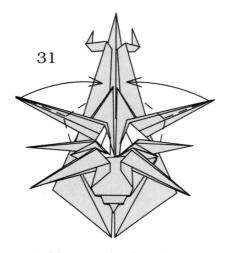

Rabbit-ear the front legs.

32

Shape the legs with simple mountain and valley folds.

33

By folding the rabbit ear, the weevil's head will point towards the ground. Sink the wings.

34

Weevil

Asparagus Beetle

This is a species of the leaf beetle family. The adult and its larvae cause much damage to the asparagus plant. The adults hibernate in old asparagus stalks. In the spring they come out and feed on the young shoots of the new asparagus. Then the female lays tiny black eggs on the stalk. The beetles, about six millimeters long, are blue and black and have yellow spots on their wings, and have a reddish thorax.

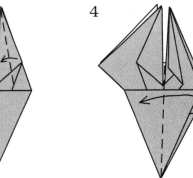

Begin with step 7 of the weevil (page 96).

1

Squash-fold.

2

Petal-fold.

3

4

5

6

7

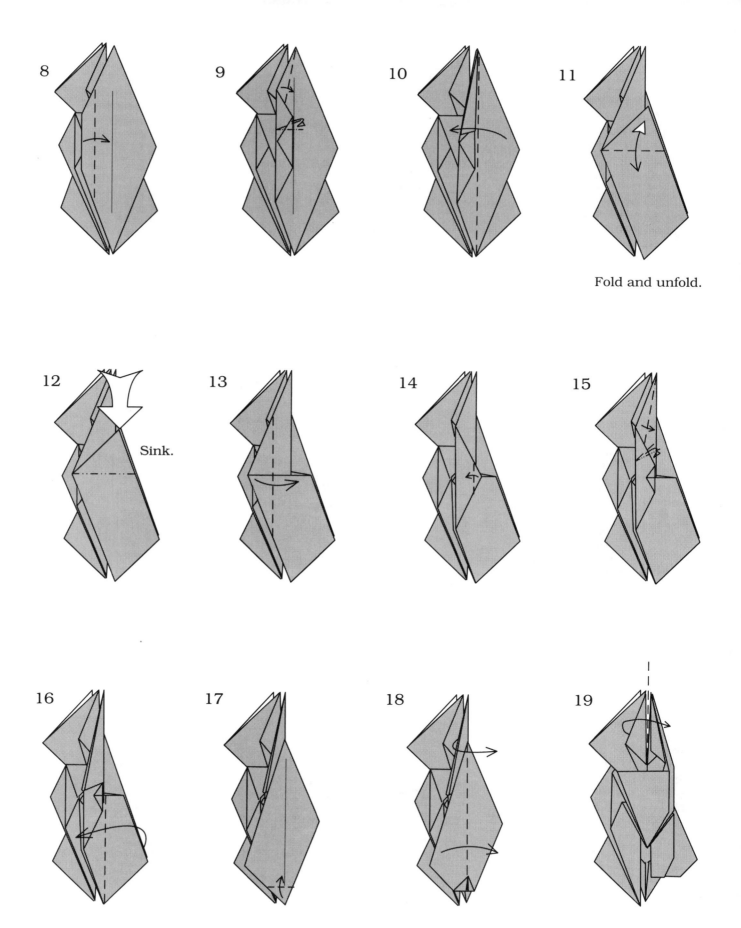

8

9

10

11

Fold and unfold.

12

Sink.

13

14

15

16

17

18

19

20

Repeat steps
1–19 on the left.

21

Place the darker
paper on top.

22

1. Tuck inside.
2. Fold behind.
3. Fold behind and unfold.

23

Sink.

24 Head.

Squash-fold
the eyes.

25

1. Shape the antennae
   with reverse folds.
2. Fold the eyes.
3. Make the neck
   three-dimensional.

Fold the legs and tail as in
the weevil (steps 22–32 of the
weevil) but treat the front legs
as the other ones (that is,
omit steps 28 and 31).

26

Asparagus beetle

Panda

The Giant Panda is a rare animal found in dense bamboo jungles in Western China and Tibet at elevations of 6000 to 14000 feet. Adults are about six feet long and weigh 300 pounds. In its environment of snow and black rocks, its white and black coloring acts as a camoflauge. It is agile and can climb trees. This nocturnal mammal spends more than half its day eating large amounts of bamboo shoots, other plants, and sometimes small animals.

1

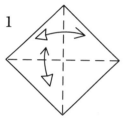

Fold and unfold along the diagonals.

2

3

4

Unfold.

5

6

7

Unfold.

8

9

10

Unfold.

11

Squash-fold.

12

13

Repeat steps
11–12 on the left.

14

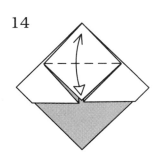

Fold up and unfold.

15

Squash-fold.

16

17

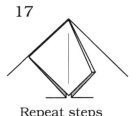

Repeat steps
15–16 on the left.

18

Petal-fold.

19

Reverse folds.

20

Squash folds.

21

22

23

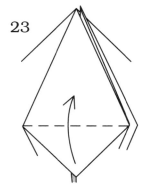

Formation
of the ears.

24

25

26

Unfold.

27

Repeat steps
24–26 on the left.

28

29

Rabbit-ear.

30

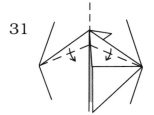

31

This fold is similar
to a rabbit ear.

32

33

34

Unlock some paper.

35

36

Unlock some paper.

37

38

39

40

Squash-fold so A
falls along line A–B.

41

42

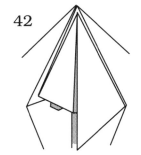

Form the other ear (repeat
steps 22–41 on the right).

43

44

Unfold.

45

Using A as a guide,
fold B down so it will
be on the line C–D.

46

Unfold.

47

48

Pull out some paper.

49

Squash-fold.

50

Pull out some paper.

51

52

Squash-fold.

53

Petal-fold.

54

55

Pull out some paper.

56

Formation of the nose.

57

Squash-fold to begin
forming the eyes.

58

Squash-fold.

59

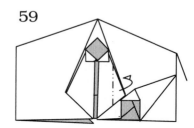

Repeat steps
57–59 on the left.

60

(The details on the
face are not drawn.)

The front legs will
now be formed.

61

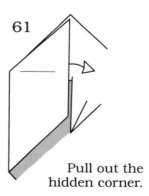

Pull out the
hidden corner.

62

63

64

65

Squash-fold.

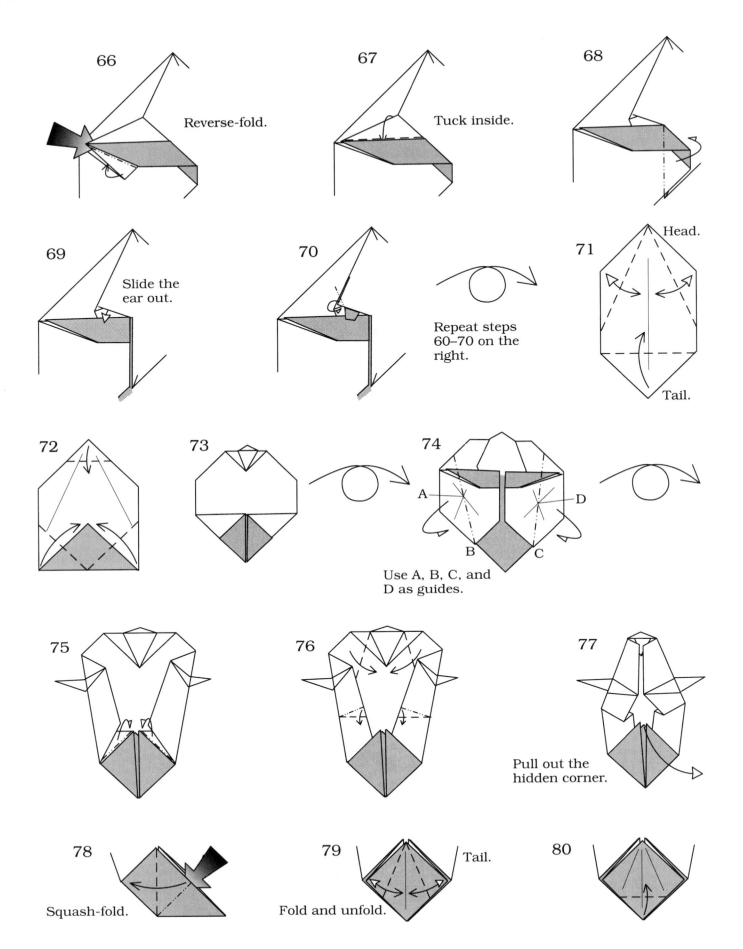

66 Reverse-fold.

67 Tuck inside.

68

69 Slide the ear out.

70 Repeat steps 60–70 on the right.

71 Head. Tail.

72

73

74 A B C D Use A, B, C, and D as guides.

75

76

77 Pull out the hidden corner.

78 Squash-fold.

79 Fold and unfold. Tail.

80

81

82

Petal-fold.

83

84

Fold the back legs down
and crimp fold the neck.

85

Repeat behind.

86

Reverse-fold.

87

1. Outside-reverse-fold the tail.
2. Pull some paper out to form
   the foot. Repeat behind.

88

Crimp-fold,
repeat behind.

89

Front
legs.

Reverse-fold,
repeat behind.

90

1. Reverse-fold.
   Repeat behind.
2. Bend at the knee.
   Repeat behind.
3. Shape the back.

91

Panda

Elephant

The largest and most powerful living land animals, elephants are six to eleven feet tall and can weigh six tons or more. The trunk is an enlongated upper lip and nose. Elephants use their trunks for gathering food, drinking, smelling, fighting, throwing dust and water over their bodies, and making trumpeting sounds. They wave their trunks around to pick up faint smells.

Elephants live in Asian and African tropics and travel in herds of a hundred or more. They eat about 500 pounds of leaves, twigs, roots, and fruits and drink 50 gallons of water a day. They can run at 25 miles an hour and are good swimmers. Though large and powerful they are gentle and graceful.

1
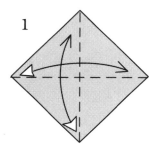

Fold and unfold along the diagonals.

2
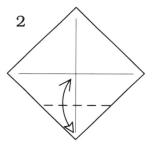

Crease lightly as you fold the bottom corner to the center and unfold.

3
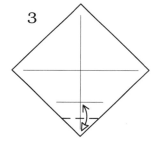

Fold to the crease and unfold.

4
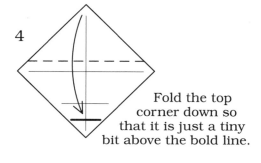

Fold the top corner down so that it is just a tiny bit above the bold line.

5

6

7

8

9

10

11

12

Unfold everything.

13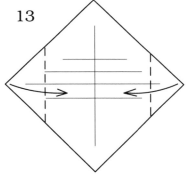

Note that there are two horizontal lines above the center and one horizontal line below. Fold on the existing creases.

14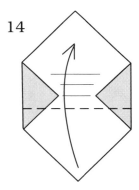

Fold up on the existing crease.

15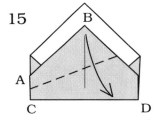

Fold down so that the corners A and B lie along the line C–D.

16

Unfold.

17

Fold and unfold.

18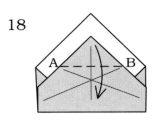

Use A and B as guides.

19

Unfold.

20

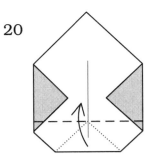

Use the hidden corner as a guide.

21

Unfold.

22

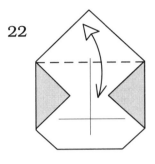

Fold down and unfold.

23

Rotate the model.

24

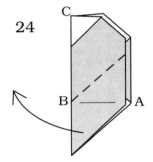

Fold so that line A–B falls along C–B.

25

Squash-fold.

26

27

Unfold and rotate the model.

28

Squash-fold.

29

30

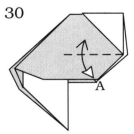

Fold point A up and unfold. Repeat behind.

31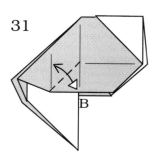

Fold B up and to
the left. Unfold and
repeat behind.

32

Fold C down and to
the left. Unfold.

33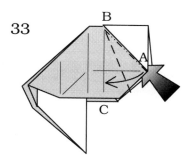

Crimp-fold corner A
to lie on the line B–C.

34

Fold line G–B
down. Unfold.

35

Squash-fold D to E. A
will fall on the line H–I.

36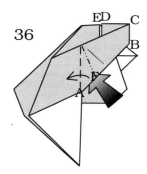

Squash-fold point
F to the left.

37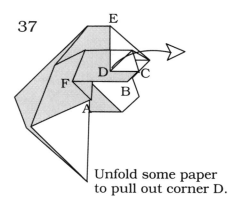

Unfold some paper
to pull out corner D.

38

39

40

41

42

Repeat steps
35–41 behind.

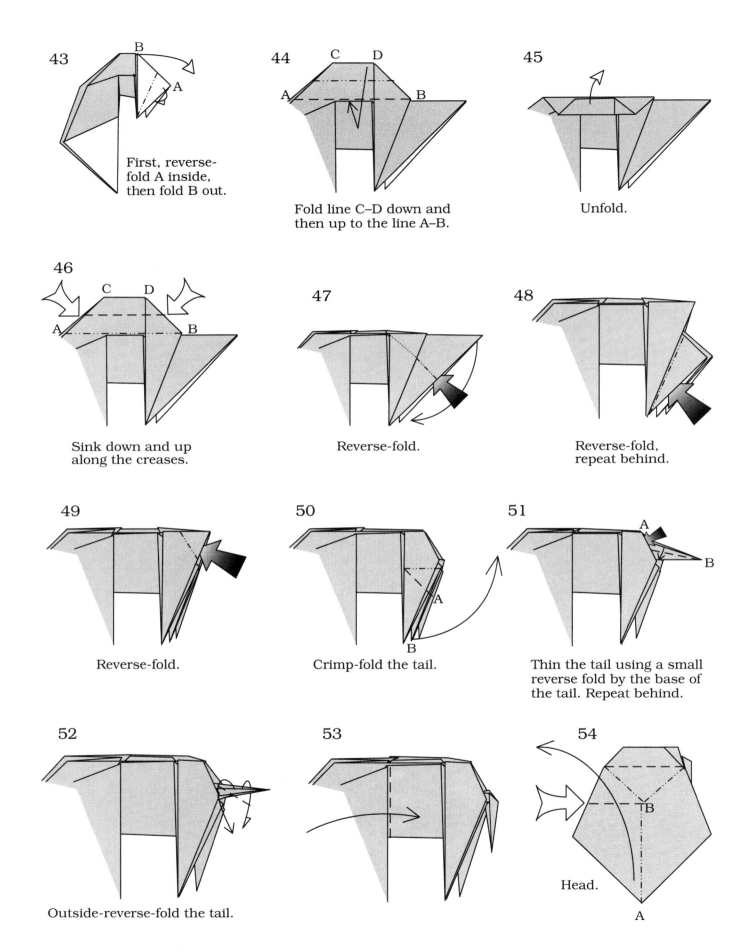

43

First, reverse-fold A inside, then fold B out.

44

Fold line C–D down and then up to the line A–B.

45

Unfold.

46

Sink down and up along the creases.

47

Reverse-fold.

48

Reverse-fold, repeat behind.

49

Reverse-fold.

50

Crimp-fold the tail.

51

Thin the tail using a small reverse fold by the base of the tail. Repeat behind.

52

Outside-reverse-fold the tail.

53

54

Head.

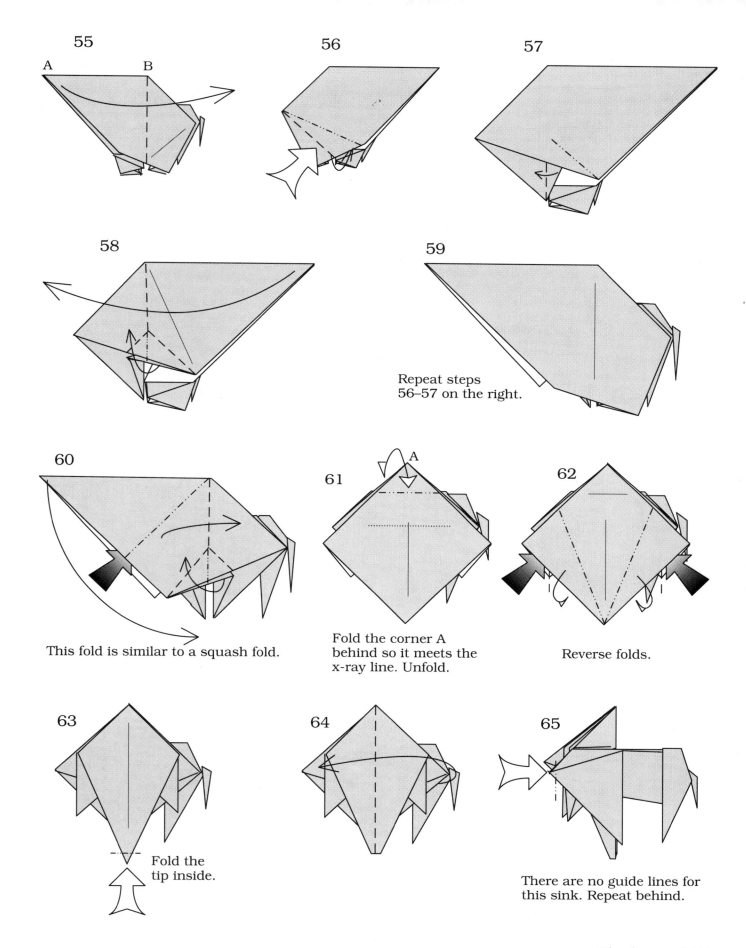

55

A · · · · · B

56

57

58

59

Repeat steps
56–57 on the right.

60

This fold is similar to a squash fold.

61

A

Fold the corner A
behind so it meets the
x-ray line. Unfold.

62

Reverse folds.

63

Fold the
tip inside.

64

65

There are no guide lines for
this sink. Repeat behind.

66

Rabbit-ear.
Repeat behind.

67

Pull out the bottom of the ears.
(Repeat behind.) Perhaps you can
skip this step since it is really easier
to go from step 66 to 68 directly.

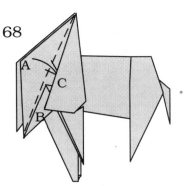

68

Fold the layer A
above B but below
C. Repeat behind.

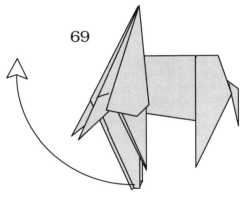

69

Pull out the trunk.

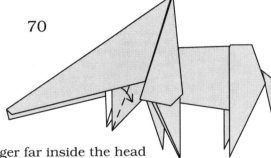

70

Place your finger far inside the head
to fold the layer in half so the tusk
will be white. Repeat behind.

71

Squash-fold.

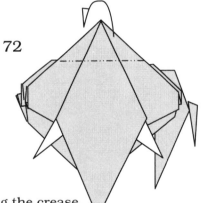

72

Tuck along the crease.

73

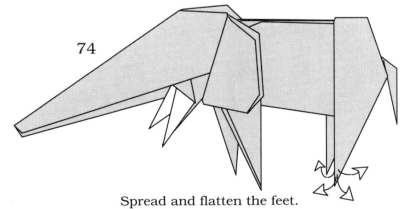

74

Spread and flatten the feet.

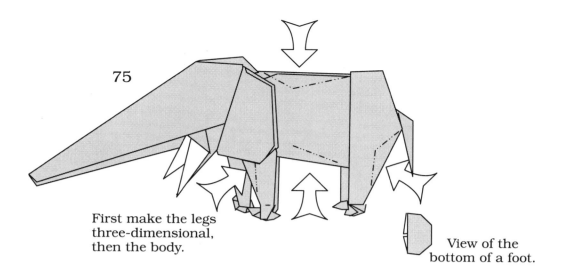

75

First make the legs
three-dimensional,
then the body.

View of the
bottom of a foot.

76

Repeat behind.

Rabbit-ear the tusks.

77

Shape the ears,
tusks, and trunk.

78

Elephant

Basic Folds

Rabbit Ear.

To fold a rabbit ear, one corner is folded in half and laid down to a side.

1

2

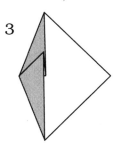

3

Fold a rabbit ear.

A three-dimensional intermediate step.

Double Rabbit Ear.

If you were to bend a straw you would be folding the double rabbit ear.

1   2

(Straw)

1

Make a double rabbit ear.

2

Squash Fold.

In a squash fold, some paper is opened and then made flat. The shaded arrow shows where to place your finger.

1

Squash-fold.

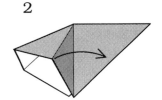

2

A three-dimensional intermediate step.

3

Petal Fold.

In a petal fold, one point is folded up while two opposite sides meet each other.

1

Petal-fold.

2

A three-dimensional intermediate step.

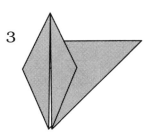

3

Inside Reverse Fold.

In an inside reverse fold, some paper is folded between layers. Here are two examples.

Reverse-fold.

Reverse-fold.

Outside Reverse Fold.

Much of the paper must be unfolded to make an outside reverse fold.

Outside-reverse-fold.

Crimp Fold.

A crimp fold is a combination of two reverse folds.

Crimp-fold.

Sink Fold.

In a sink fold, some of the paper without edges is folded inside. To do this fold, much of the model must be unfolded.

Sink.

Spread Squash Fold.

A cross between a squash fold and sink fold, some paper in the center is spread apart and then made flat.

Spread-squash-fold.